LAGOM

LAGOM

The Swedish Art of Living a Balanced, Happy Life

NIKI BRANTMARK

creator of *My Scandinavian Home*

Thorsons

Thorsons

An imprint of HarperCollins*Publishers*

1 London Bridge Street

London SE1 9GF

www.harpercollins.co.uk

First published by Thorsons 2017

10 9 8 7 6 5 4 3 2

Editorial Director: Carolyn Thorne

Design: Lucy Sykes-Thompson

Editor: Holly Kyte

Project editors: Sarah Hammond and Georgina Atsiaris

A catalogue record of this book is available from the British Library

ISBN 978-0-00-826010-1

Printed and bound in Latvia

MIX
Paper from
responsible sources
FSC™ C007454
www.fsc.org

For my family, who remind me
of what's important in life.

CONTENTS

▽

An introduction to lagom

Fourteen years ago, I was invited to spend my summer holiday with a Swedish friend.

The long hours of daylight were spent eating home-baked waffles with strawberry jam, swimming in the sea and soaking up the sun on Sweden's West Coast. The days were carefree and uncomplicated. We had no schedule to keep, no fancy meals to prepare and work couldn't have been further from our minds. It was about slowing down, enjoying the warmer weather and making the most of what nature had to offer, surrounded by family and friends. It was the perfect setting for the beginnings of a love affair – not only with my Swedish husband but also with the Swedish way of life.

I found myself captivated by this slower, fuss-free way of living. And when my husband and I discussed who should make the 'big move' one year later, I was on my way to the airport faster than I could say 'Jag!' (me!).

As I settled into Swedish life, I realized that the calm approach isn't confined to the holidays. At work, it's normal to set tasks aside regularly and take a *fika* (a break involving a coffee and a treat of some kind). Children enjoy two extra years of play before starting school (compared to their UK counterparts). And celebrations like Christmas and midsummer are generally scaled-back affairs with a strong focus on being together. In other words, our Nordic friends take their time to do things right – in a wonderful, uncomplicated way.

It was at a dinner party in my adopted hometown of Malmö that I learnt the philosophy behind this way of life.

'Do you know the word lagom?' my new Swedish friends asked over dinner. 'You don't have a translation for it in English,' they said proudly.

'Does it mean "perfect"?' I ventured.

'No, not perfect – it's sort of "just right",' they explained, nodding in agreement with each other.

Lagom, pronounced 'lah-gom' ('la' like 'far', 'gom' like 'from'), is an overarching concept that is heavily ingrained in the Swedish psyche. Often loosely translated as 'everything 'in moderation' or 'not too much and not too little', lagom is about finding a balance that works for you. Water can be lagom warm. You can work a lagom amount. Trousers can be a lagom fit. It's a word you can use in almost any context, which is also what makes it fascinating.

Lagom is commonly thought to derive from Viking times, rooted in the term *laget om* (around the team). It's said a bowl or horn of mead would be passed in a circle, and it was important that everyone only sipped their 'fair share' so there was enough to go round. The Vikings wouldn't usually be first on my list as a moral compass, but they were certainly on to something. Today, lagom is closely linked to the Swedish cultural and social ideology of fairness and equality. Ferociously independent they may be, but Swedes are also known for working together for the collective good. Taking the 'right amount' is a step towards ensuring that no one amasses too much and no one is left wanting.

Whether it's applied to work, leisure, family and relationships, holidays and celebrations, interior design or living in a way that's kinder to the planet, the Swedes will often tell you that *lagom är bäst* – the right amount is best, and moderation is key.

Having said that, there's definitely a time for excess in Sweden. If you've ever been to a Swedish midsummer celebration or drunk a cup of their (exceedingly strong) freshly brewed coffee, you'll know what I mean. It's just that they won't punish themselves with abstinence afterwards. The Swede will simply continue enjoying everything in moderation (until the next celebration comes along!).

By deliberately seeking a more manageable, comfortable, balanced way of doing things (and finding perfection in imperfection), you're not just taking the pressure off yourself – you're taking the pressure off others, too. And you're gaining more of today's most precious resource: time.

In a world where we're connected 24/7 and have so much on our plates, wouldn't it be wonderful if we could all slow down a little and lead a life with less stress and more time for the things we love?

You are no doubt exercising lagom in many aspects of your life already. However, I hope the ideas in this book will help you think more consciously about introducing lagom in other ways, too; in a way that works for you. By making subtle changes to your everyday routine, you can find greater balance – and make time for the things that matter most in life. Even if it's just taking time out of your day to enjoy a *fika*!

01

Lagom
in your
personal
life

the lagom home

Happiness begins at home (or is that charity?). Either way, research shows that our environment affects our stress levels,[1] which in turn affects our physical well-being. After all, home is where we start and end our day. And, in my mind, if there's one area where Swedes have truly triumphed, it's in the home. The typical Scandinavian home is the very essence of lagom. It's neither too sparse nor too fussy, neither overly minimalist nor overdone. In other words, Swedes have the balance just right. But how?

When it comes to decor, our Nordic friends exercise a huge amount of restraint. Walls are often white or light grey. Not only do these muted tones brighten the space but they also create a wonderfully serene feel. Nothing brash, nothing loud, no bold patterns – just calm.

Furniture and accessories are carefully thought out, too. New pieces are chosen for practicality as well as aesthetic appeal. Nothing is superfluous, with no frills or over-the-top designs. Single items are set apart to give them breathing space, helping the eye see the beauty in every piece. Ultimately, the home becomes a little oasis, a haven from the busy world outside.

CLEAN +
CLUTTER-FREE

Generally speaking, Swedes have a natural ability to maintain an uncluttered home. They simply don't have much stuff and they don't hoard. If we wish to achieve a simple, balanced lagom way of life, we first need to rid ourselves of all the things that clutter our homes.

Signs you need to de-clutter

+ You have an entire cupboard or room for items you never use.

+ Or, you wish you had an extra room for storing your clutter.

+ It takes you more than five minutes to find something you're looking for.

+ You feel stressed at the thought of friends coming over (or, worse still, turning up unannounced) because you have so much to clear away first.

+ You own items you neither use nor find joy in.

You may be lucky enough to have a neat and tidy haven already, in which case – congratulations! You're well on your way to a lagom life (in the home, at least). But if you checked more than one of the boxes above, there's work to be done.

De-cluttering

Many of us are guilty of owning too much stuff. That cupboard with boxes of photos circa 1984, old mobile phones the size of a brick, keys for the garden shed at your last house. We've become a world of hoarders, because, let's face it, it's very hard to let go of things. Maybe you bought it because you thought you'd need it at some point. It may still have a price tag on it, and you feel guilty about getting rid of something brand new. Or you may have received a gift or inherited something you know you'll never use but can't bring yourself to throw away. No matter the reason, these items are cluttering up your home and having a negative effect on your well-being.

Scientists list distraction, anxiety, guilt, embarrassment and frustration among the negative effects of hoarding. Furthermore, clutter makes it harder for us to relax and inhibits our creativity. *Yikes!*

Ultimately, de-cluttering is an exercise in willpower and self-control, but it's certainly not impossible. And it can also be an incredibly therapeutic process. Not only do you experience direct financial, emotional and physical benefits but it also paves the way to a blissfully neat and tidy home. So, let's get started.

'Have nothing in your houses that you do not know to be useful, or believe to be beautiful.'

William Morris

Ten simple ways to de-clutter your home

Create a de-clutter to-do list, crossing off each task as you complete it.

Dedicate ten minutes each day to one task (baby steps, my friend).

Go one room at a time and organize items into three boxes: keep, donate and throw away (never a 'maybe' box – speaking from experience!).

Follow the 'one in, one out' rule – for everything you buy, one thing goes.

Fill a bin bag a day with items you no longer need.

Reduce the area where clutter can accumulate – dedicate a container for toiletries or a folder for paperwork. If new items don't fit, then it's time to re-think what's in the area and get rid of something.

Take out all the items in your wardrobe. Remove five hangers and then put everything back in order of preference. Anything that doesn't have a hanger goes.

Create a memory box or use an accordion organizer for your kids' drawings and other treasured items.

Keep a basket or bag by the stairs or in a spot that accumulates clutter and slowly fill it with items. Once it's full, sort through and put everything back where it belongs.

Stick to the 'one-touch rule' for paperwork: sort it as soon as it arrives by recycling, filing or taking action.

FURNISHING YOUR HOME, THE LAGOM WAY

Swedes have an innate ability to furnish a home in a way that's practical, easy on the eye and affordable. The art, I've discovered, is slowing down and taking your time to search for meaningful, purposeful items, such as a comfortable, ergonomic chair for a quiet read, plants that help clean the air or an ornament that puts a smile on your face.

Step inside a Swedish home and you'll likely discover a selection of high-street pieces, vintage and secondhand finds, hand-me-downs, homemade items and small treasures from nature, such as plants, pebbles, shells and pine cones. The materials are honest, and the shapes timeless.

By buying less and carefully selecting what to include in your home, everything has space to shine and tell its story. And because of your patience in seeking beautifully crafted items with meaning, you will treasure them for years to come – as will future generations, too!

New is not necessarily better

As a naturally nosy person (and a lover of interiors), you can imagine how thrilled I was to learn about the Swedish custom of giving a guided home tour the first time someone visits. While on these tours, it struck me that Swedes have a knack for blending furniture. I particularly admire those who create the ideal balance of old and new, vintage and modern. It's a perfectly understated way of decorating and is very much in line with the Swedish mind-set. An expensive designer lamp or armchair will be offset by a mid-century credenza to ensure the home is neither too showy nor too bohemian. Of course, it's fine to own a few designer pieces, but everything should be in moderation.

In my mind, nothing makes a home cosier (or *mysigare*, as the Swedes would say) and unique than vintage pieces. Not only do they tell a story but you also feel satisfied knowing that you're doing your bit for mother earth. And it's amazing what you can pick up secondhand for a song, truly reinforcing the idea that 'One man's loss is another man's treasure!'

Six tips for buying secondhand

Make a list (or two) Include secondhand stores, flea markets and car-boot sales in your neighbourhood. And think further afield, too, because smaller, out-of-town flea markets are often where you find the biggest bargains. Make a note of the items you're looking to buy, too.

Check the condition Try to see the item in person so you can check for damage. If it's not possible, request photos of any nicks or scratches and ask whether it's in full working order.

Measure first Make sure you know the exact dimensions of the space where you're thinking of putting the item and take the measurements with you.

Be flexible You might not find exactly what you're looking for, but something else equally wonderful might pop up.

Arrive early and bring cash The best things go first, so be ready to buy immediately. If you're unsure about a price, check online for similar items to compare.

Turn it into a day out Even if you don't find anything, a mini road trip with a friend is always fun.

Get flexible

If a brand were to be the embodiment of lagom, it's IKEA
– a company founded, of course, in Sweden. With a vision 'to
create a better everyday life for the many people', the furniture
marries function with understated form and is famous for
being flat-pack and affordable.

IKEA is not alone in producing increasingly multi-
purpose furniture. For example, it's not uncommon these days
for a sofa to be modular, include built-in storage and convert
into a bed, or for a side table to feature a removable tray and
basket for magazines. By investing in multi-purpose furniture,
you automatically purchase fewer pieces (and consequently
save money) and have a more flexible home.

Think practical

Your home has to be highly functional for you to feel happy
and relaxed. Above all, it should be easy to live in. Swedes
are masters at carving out distinct zones for living, eating
and sleeping – even in the smallest spaces. Think about your
requirements and try to have a space (no matter how small)
dedicated to different activities. You might find that two areas
can double up as one.

Tap into your inner carpenter

The cheaper and self-sufficient option, DIY is part of the lagom way of life. My Swedish husband laid our wood floor without so much as an expletive, and it's not unusual for one of my girlfriends to whip out her toolbox when something needs fixing. Although I'm still an amateur, I find DIY liberating, satisfying and surprisingly mindful. If you don't have one already, I urge you to buy a toolbox, look for guidelines online and unleash your inner carpenter!

CREATE A **TOOL WALL**

▽

If you like having your tools to hand, creating a dedicated tool wall in your study or garage is not only extremely handy, but can also look pretty cool. All you need is a pegboard, which you can get at any large DIY store, and accessories to hold everything from scissors and sticky tape to heavy-duty tools. Your inner creative will thank you for it!

Get crafty

I am continually amazed at how creative the Swedes are – they're a real dab hand at upcycling and making things from scratch. Cooking and baking is one thing, but some of the items my friends knock up are awe-inspiring. Knitted cushions, handcrafted trays, even lamps and entire kitchens are pulled off at the whirl of an electric drill.

You see, arts and crafts are in a Swede's DNA. As children, they've seen their parents sit and create, and they hone their skills at school where everyone learns to sew, cook and do woodwork. These days it's referred to as 'slow living', an antidote to our busy 24/7 lives. Not only are creative tasks incredibly mindful but they're also therapeutic and highly satisfying. Here are some ways you can get creative in the home:

The simple update

Thinking of throwing out a table or sideboard? How about giving it a lick of paint or new handle pulls instead? A new colour could give it just the look you're after, and by adding some new leather or ceramic handles, the update can instantly give the space a fresh feel.

HOW TO MAKE
A VASE OUT OF A
REPURPOSED LIGHT BULB

This DIY idea not only looks beautiful but it's also easy to make and won't cost you a penny!

What you need

+ Eye protection
+ Pliers
+ A light bulb
+ Scissors
+ Twine or fishing wire

1. Don your eye protection, then use pliers to remove the metal tab at the base of the light bulb.

2. Hold the metal base and carefully break the glass inside the base of the bulb. Remove all glass fragments.

3. Hold the bulb by the metal base and use pliers to break the glass surrounding the filament. Remove the glass and filament.

4. Cut the twine to the desired length and tie around the base of the bulb.

5. Add water and fresh flowers (or any decoration that takes your fancy) and hang your bulb vase in the window.

GET COSY AND CLOSER TO NATURE

There's a stereotype that minimalism is cold and uninviting. But with a little creativity, it's easy to overcome. As you can imagine, Swedes have this down to a fine art, and much of their secret lies in their use of nature. With acres of unspoiled forests, coastline and mountains on their doorstep, it's common to use plenty of natural texture in the Swedish home. Think materials that are sensory to the touch, such as wood, leather, felt, wool and stone. Sheepskin throws are draped over the backs of chairs; wool blankets are waiting to be unfurled at the slightest sign of a draught; cotton rugs are dotted about the floor.

When you decorate your home, why not learn from the Swedes and think about adding natural materials with different structures and textures? It's amazing how much warmth a simple wooden coffee table or sheepskin throw can add to an otherwise minimalist space.

Bring nature indoors

If you'd really like to up the nature stakes, go for a forage and collect wild flowers, feathers, sticks, pine cones, pebbles, shells and anything else you might find on the beach, in the woods or simply growing through cracks in the pavement. Display them in your home on a windowsill, shelf or as a centrepiece on the dining table to create an instant connection with the great outdoors and add a sense of balance and calm.

Six house plants that will survive anything

Look in any Swedish home and you'll see plants lining the windowsills and brightening up dark corners. They're certainly on to something. Studies have shown that having just one plant in a room can ease stress levels, absorb harmful toxins and help purify the air. It can also help enhance your mood and increase productivity,[2] boost concentration and memory and, ultimately, make you feel happier. It's also a wonderful way to bring the home alive.

+ Rubber tree plant   **+ Snake plant**

+ Madagascar dragon tree

+ Spider plant

+ Aloe vera plant

+ Fiddle leaf fig tree

More than just a plant

For many people, plants are more than just a bit of greenery –
they're a living friend. I'm a little embarrassed to admit that
some of our plants have names, and according to friends I'm
not alone. Our most treasured plant started life as a cutting
from one of my grandfather-in-law's shrubs. Sadly, he's long
since gone, but the plant lives on in his memory.

Why not get a cutting from a friend's or relative's plant,
or give one as a present to mark an occasion? Not only is it free
but it'll also hold special memories. You never know, it might
live on for generations to come!

Keeping it simple

Instead of displaying a huge bouquet, think about placing a single flower in a vase. You'll more easily be able to admire its delicate shape and colour.

Think outside the vase

Having a get-together? How about giving the wall a natural touch by sticking on blooms from your garden? It creates an instant seasonal display.

Or, for something more permanent, pick a selection of your favourite leaves and place them inside double-sided glass frames. These look beautiful on the wall or arranged along a windowsill.

'Sometimes a single, modest bloom can say more than an entire bouquet.'

Ilkka Suppanen, Finnish designer at be&liv

THREE CREATIVE WAYS
TO TURN NATURE INTO MEMORIES

It's wonderful to experience the great outdoors first hand, but if you're stuck inside you can still reap the benefits. A study led by VU University Medical Center in the Netherlands found that simply viewing images of nature reduces our stress levels.[3]

These lovely ideas below not only help to combat stress (if the study is anything to go by) but also take us back in time to a magical place where we felt happy and relaxed:

+ **Create a gallery wall** using a montage of photographs of sunsets you've enjoyed on holiday. Make sure each one is labelled with the place and date to jolt your memory and transport you back in time.

+ **Love to surf,** paddleboard or simply chill on the beach? Why not bring back a small sample of sand, put it into a glass bottle and mark it with the name of the beach? The different colour sands make a pretty display and serve as a wonderful reminder of carefree days at the water's edge.

+ **Put up a picture** of a landscape that you love – a seascape from your childhood, fields at harvest time or a forest you enjoy going to at the weekends.

LET THERE BE LIGHT!

Living in a country as famous for its midnight sun as its long, dark winters, it's little wonder the Swedes are obsessed with light. Whereas warmer countries design homes around shade, Scandinavian architecture and decor focus on maximizing light and drawing it inside.

Windows are left unobscured, and curtains are often sheer so as to slip in as much natural light as possible. White or pale grey walls help light to bounce around the home. And it seems the Swedes are on to something. A slew of studies has shown that access to natural light can help reduce depression,[4] aid recovery, increase job satisfaction and enhance performance. So let the sunshine in!

Let there be darkness, too!

With all this natural light streaming in through the windows 24 hours a day in summer, you might wonder how Swedes get any sleep at all. But look closely at any window and you'll usually see a tightly rolled blackout blind, ready to be unfurled at night (desperate for light they may be, but Swedes would never deprive themselves of all-important sleep!).

Lighting-up time

Walk around a Swedish town at night and you'll notice restaurants, cafés and people's homes lit with a lovely warm glow, which is as inviting as it is flattering to the eye and soothing to the soul. Swedes' innate ability to light a home with a soft, golden hue takes time and dedication, but there are a few shortcuts you can take. If you're looking to dial down the lighting in your home – or are entertaining a Swede anytime soon (get it wrong and they'll wince and grimace like a bear waking up after winter) – there are simple steps you can take. We're focusing on ambient or mood lighting, designed to create a warm and inviting atmosphere. Candlelight is akin to 1,500 K (kelvin) and overcast daylight is around 7,000 K, so you're looking at a 2,700 K light bulb to achieve a warm tone similar to the beautiful, flattering golden light you find at sunrise.

The good news is most LED light-bulb packaging is marked with a colour temperature chart, where reddish-yellow light suggests soft, ambient lighting and blue indicates a colder, more intense light used for specific tasks.

Once you've got your light bulbs down to a tee, here's the trick: keep upper walls relatively dark and then use low, soft ambient lighting in strategic places. Or go a step further and hide the ambient lighting so there's no visible source, yet the lower walls and corners of the room are still lit in soft, warm light, to create an intimate feel with a touch of mystery.

Colour temperatures on the kelvin scale

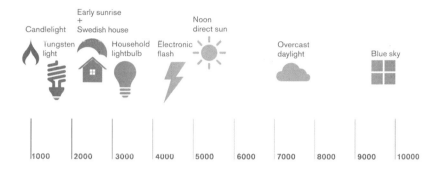

Candlelight

Tungsten
light

Early sunrise
+
Swedish house

Household
lightbulb

Noon
direct sun

Electronic
flash

Overcast
daylight

Blue sky

| 1000 | 2000 | 3000 | 4000 | 5000 | 6000 | 7000 | 8000 | 9000 | 10000 |

Practical lighting

Don't forget that Swedes are highly practical, too. It's therefore important that a room's lighting is adequate for all tasks. Think carefully about the way each section of the room will be used and ensure the correct blend of task, overhead and ambient lighting. Exchanging static switches for dimmers[5] is a great way to use the same light for more than one purpose. Dial down the intensity for mood lighting, or ramp it up for tasks that require something more intense, like reading.

<u>Candlelight</u>

Who doesn't love the romantic glow of a flickering candle? This soft, warm light is neither too dark nor eye-glaringly bright and perfectly highlights the contours of a face. It's little wonder that candlelight is used in restaurants or on special occasions all over the world.

In Sweden candles are a big part of daily life. A single flickering candle may be on the breakfast table to brighten dark mornings. Or candles may supplement electric lighting on chilly evenings when the snow falls silently outside.

When the light starts to fade, why not add a few strategically placed candles to your own home to soothe the soul? Dot them around your living area, enjoy a candle-lit dinner on a regular Tuesday or simply brighten up an otherwise dark corner and feel the stresses of the day fall away.

The lagom way
with candlelight

Morning coffee by candlelight
Some days the sun simply doesn't
want to come out (especially in the
winter). At my daughter's nursery, they
often eat breakfast by candlelight –
creating a calm and cosy atmosphere
to start the day. Why not add a natural
glow to your mornings, too? Who
wouldn't enjoy coffee by candlelight?

The art of arranging candles
According to etiquette, you should
use at least two candelabras or four
single candles on a table. But rules
are there to be broken, right? I think
it's beautiful to dot small tea lights in
random formations along the entire
length of a table. On warm evenings,
hang jam jars with tea lights from
branches to give a lovely rustic touch
to dining al fresco.

Candles in unexpected places
Candles don't need to be confined
to the sitting and dining rooms. Think
about putting them in unusual places
like by the sink in the downstairs
bathroom – guests will be pleasantly
surprised to powder their nose under
the soft glow of a candle.

A warm welcome The next time
you have a dinner party or celebration,
place simple large, outdoor candles
on either side of your front door for
an extra warm welcome.

KEEP IT CLEAN

Whenever friends or family come to visit, they marvel at how spotless Swedish homes are. There's rarely a speck of dust, never mind a cobweb or trail of mud, in sight (my messier Swedish friends may guffaw at this, but I stand by my observation).

The art of being a domestic god or goddess in the cleaning department would require an entire chapter to itself (and given my more, shall we say, 'relaxed' approach, I wouldn't be the best person to write it!). But there are two particularly 'clean' Scandinavian practices that have inspired me:

Look, no shoes!

If there's one big no-no in Sweden, it's entering a house with shoes on. Whether you're nipping in for a cup of coffee or a formal evening reception, there are no exceptions. Arrive at a house party and you'll see neat rows of shoes lined up at the door and people mingling in their socks.

If you think about it, it makes sense. An independent study by UK firm Rug Doctor[6] took swabs from a cross-section of shoe soles and found a large number of disease-inducing bacteria, such as E. coli and salmonella, as well as traces of gut and faeces bacteria from humans and animals. Not to mention mud, grime and everyday germs.

Removing shoes is also a good way to preserve your flooring and carpets, and if you live above someone, they'll be extremely thankful not to hear the clip-clopping of heels overhead, too!

Out with the carpet, in with the rug

The one thing you'll never see in a Swedish home is wall-to-wall carpet. 'But they're cosy,' I lament. 'They're so unhygienic!' Swedes grimace. And they do have a point.

Your best shot at keeping a carpet clean is a good vacuum cleaner or a specialist deep-cleaning agent. Rugs, on the other hand, can be beaten outside, put through the washing machine or taken to the dry-cleaner. Plus, they're easy to move around and exchange at will – win-win!

The humble rag rug

Look around a Swedish home (particularly a rural dwelling) and you're more than likely to come across a *trasmatta*, or rag rug. This traditional rug is usually handmade on a loom from scraps of worn-out clothes and old rags. You can easily find a *trasmatta* in the shops, but why not give your old textiles a new lease of life and create your own? They're great fun to make, and if you don't happen to have an old loom knocking about, you can use a crochet stitch – there are plenty of YouTube videos showing you how.

A treat for your feet

If you like having something soft underfoot but also like a clean and dust-free home, how about layering rugs to create a complete floor covering? Stick to similar tones but with different patterns to create your very own floor art.

The lagom guide to soothing the soul

Sleep is nature's way of helping us to de-clutter the mind and restore our body and soul. Without enough of it we function less effectively, damaging our health and well-being in the long run. But it's not just a great night's sleep that creates a balanced state of mind. While I've lived in Sweden, I've grown to appreciate that slowing down and enjoying humble activities – like relaxing in a sauna and being outdoors – allows you to to switch off, live in the moment and enjoy the small things in life. I've also learnt that a back-to-basics holiday, requiring little planning or budget, can be the antidote to a world that's constantly stressful.

SLEEP

There's a lot to be said for a great night's sleep. You know, those mornings when you wake up rested and raring to go? I'm told there are several key factors involved in creating a calming pre-bedtime ritual, and in my mind the Swedes do a whole lot right in the bedroom department (after all, they're the ones who start the day eye-wateringly early).

So, what's their secret? Helena Kubicek Boye, Swedish psychologist and author of *The Art of Sleep* and *The Three Balloons* (a sleep story for children), says you need to prepare yourself both physically and mentally before going to bed.

'A ruffled mind makes a restless pillow.'

Charlotte Brontë

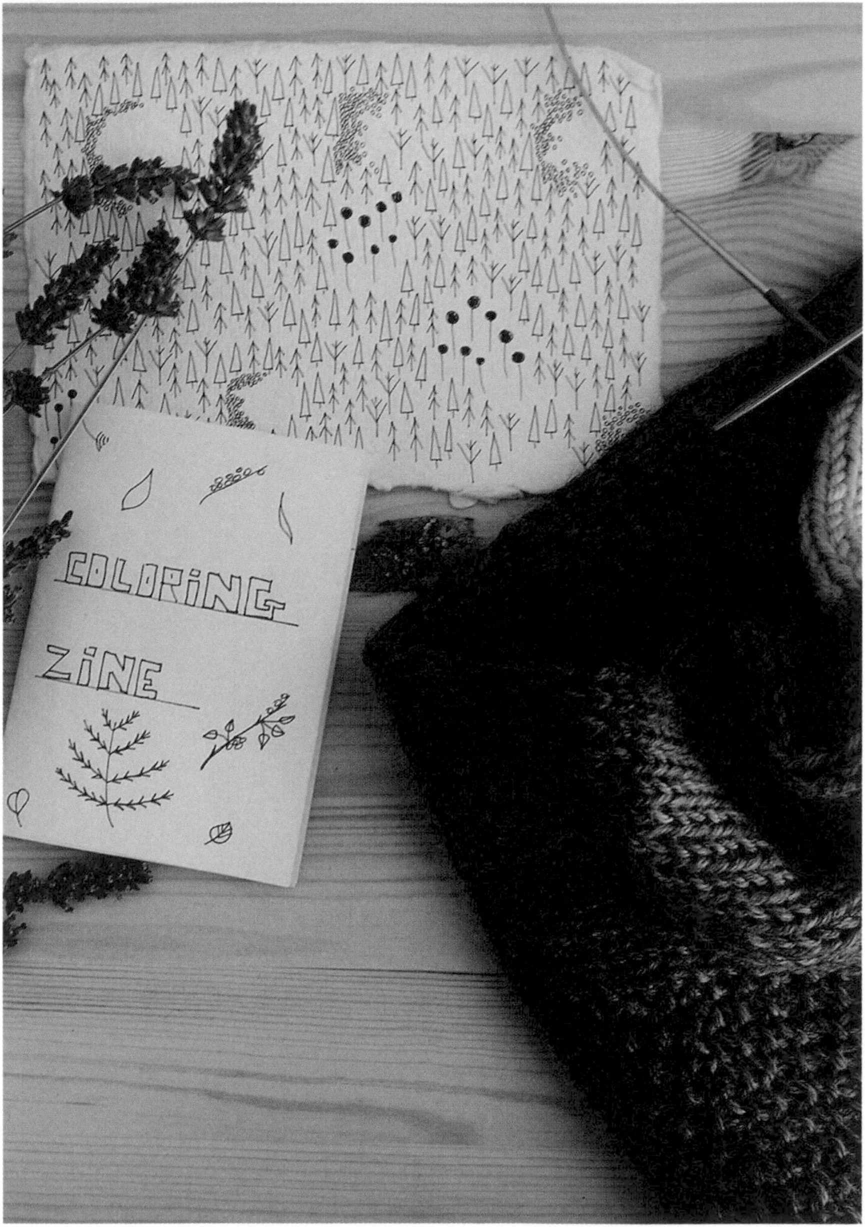
COLORING
ZINE

Preparing the mind

What you do mentally before you go to bed is key to a restful slumber. 'On the whole, your bed should be used for sex and sleep,' advises Kubicek Boye. It's advised that everything else should stay out of the bedroom.

So stalking ex-boyfriends on Facebook isn't OK? It seems not. Not only will a scroll through your favourite social-media feed before bed likely lead to a serious case of FOMO, but it will also hinder your beauty sleep. A recent study[7] in Norway found that screen light affects your ability to fall asleep and reduces the quality of your slumber. Experts recommend you avoid using any screen for up to an hour before bedtime.

So now that binge-watching the latest series on Netflix is out of the question, what should we be doing before bed?

Pre-bedtime activities

When it comes to sleep-inducing activities, Kubicek Boye lists plenty of the usual things, and a few good old-fashioned analogue activities, too:

+ reading a book
+ taking a warm bath
+ listening to calm music
+ knitting

+ embroidery
+ painting (or mindful colouring)
+ cuddling up with family and pets

Keep a diary

Often when the lights go out, thoughts and worries from the day
creep in. Keeping a journal is a great way to reflect on the events of
the day, offload niggling worries and clear your mind before sleep.

The *kvällspromenad*

> mångata (n.): The glimmering, roadlike reflection
> the moon creates on water.

It's not uncommon to take a *kvällspromenad*, or evening walk,
in Sweden — even if you don't have a dog. It usually takes
place sometime after supper and involves an amble around the
neighbourhood. It's a great way to relax and, depending on the
weather, cools down your body temperature, naturally preparing
you for sleep. Plus, if you live near water, it also gives you the
opportunity to gaze at the *mångata*, a Swedish term for the beautiful
trail of moonlight reflected on water.

Five ways to sleep
like a Swede

Go *au naturel* Swedes commonly shun traditional nightwear in favour of underwear – or simply nothing at all. Not only are Swedish homes incredibly well insulated but sleeping in less also helps keep you cool. And this improves the quality of your sleep.

Divide and conquer Book yourself into a Swedish hotel and you'll be surprised to find two single duvets instead of a double – and I've found this to be universal across all Swedish marital beds. Friends tell me that this allows you to choose a duvet cover with a thickness that's lagom for you and means you can stick out naked limbs at whim.

Keep it clean Ensure your bedroom is clutter-free, and avoid busy patterns in the decor.

Keep it calm The Swedish bedroom, with its soft, muted colour palette, minimalist furnishings and airy feel, is the epitome of calm. Think white and light grey walls, pure linen bedding (great for keeping you cool in summer and warm in winter) and layers of natural texture for cooler evenings. It's a simple space and a calming oasis in which to switch off from the stresses and strains of daily life.

Create darkness The sleep-inducing hormone melatonin is connected to the stimulation around us. By darkening your room, you're telling your body it's time to go to sleep. Use blackout blinds and cover any LED lights.

THE MORNING DIP

Blessed with 11,500km (over 7,000 miles) of coastline (not including the islands) and around 100,000 lakes, it's little wonder the Swedes love to bathe. But one type of al fresco bathing stands out: the *morgondopp*, or morning dip. Most commonly enjoyed between May and September (although some hardy types go year-round), the *morgondopp* is usually enjoyed first thing in the morning before coffee. The bather dons a dressing gown and wanders down to the local bathing deck.

The length of time you stay in the water depends on the temperature, which I've noticed is something of a national obsession. Bathing piers wouldn't be complete without a small thermometer bobbing on the end of a string. Some people decide their bathing 'season' around these numbers. For example, my parents-in-law, Inger and Bo, begin their season when the mercury rises above 10°C (50°F)! 'As soon as I hit the water, I feel completely awake and ready for the day ahead,' enthuses Inger. 'It's just you and the great expanse of water. It's an incredibly humbling experience and so relaxing to feel the warm sun and cool breeze on your body afterwards.'

No excuses!

Nowhere near any sea, river, stream or lake? Try ending your daily shower with a cold-water blast. It may not be as mindful or empowering as a saltwater swim, but you'll still get many of the physiological benefits and will almost certainly wake up with a jolt!

'She loved the sea.
She liked the sharp, salty
smell of the air, and the
vastness of the horizons,
bounded only by a vault of
azure sky above. It made her
feel small, but free as well.'

George R. R. Martin
A Storm of Swords

Five great reasons to enjoy a morning dip

Boost your immunity A study by Czech scientists found that immersing your body in cold water daily indicated an increased number of white blood cells in your body.[8] These activate your immune system and boost your health.

Get a natural high and relieve pain When you jump into cold water, your body releases endorphins in reaction to the burning sensation on your skin. This rush also acts as an anti-inflammatory, momentarily eliminating aches and pains.

Relieve allergies Hay fever sufferers (of which I am one) will be interested to hear that sea water acts as a natural nasal decongestant, cleansing pollen from nasal passages without irritating the skin.

Boost your sex life As if I haven't given you reason enough! Immersing yourself in cold water is said to increase testosterone and oestrogen, which boosts the libido.

Get happy A study[9] by Virginia Commonwealth University School of Medicine found that submerging yourself in cold water could have antidepressive effects.

See you at the water's edge!

How to enter cold water – from a year-round bather

'Instead of thinking how cold it's going to be, the key is to relax and focus on positive factors, such as the beautiful scenery, the stillness of the ocean, the formation of birds as they swoop across the sky, or the freedom you'll feel once you're in the water.'

Maibritt Johnsson, Malmö, Sweden

SAUNA

Ask people for a word associated with Sweden and 'sauna' will likely pop up high on the list. Simply referred to locally as *bada bastu*, or a casual *basta*, sauna use varies widely across the country. There are avid users who choose to go alone, arriving at the crack of dawn to enjoy the peace and tranquillity. Others use the session to catch up with a friend, and there are even whole groups who meet as part of a monthly sauna club (my husband being one).

Either way, the routine is generally the same. The idea of the *bada bastu* is to perspire *au naturel* in hot, dry heat in a small wood-lined room until you feel the need to cool off. You then submerge your body in cold water (whether that's a dip in the sea, a cold shower or a roll in the snow – brrrrrr!) and relax for a while in the great outdoors before repeating the process (usually up to three times).

Although some people enjoy private saunas, most large towns in Sweden have a public sauna – it's a bit of an institution. A British friend once observed that the public sauna is 'the closest thing the Swedes have to the local village pub'. It's an establishment where everyone's welcome, prejudices are stripped away at the door (along with clothes), and people of all ages and backgrounds sit together in harmony.

The 'nude' aspect of the Swedish sauna may leave the more prudish among us positively squirming. But, hygiene factors aside, going in your birthday suit enhances the wonderful, unpretentious nature of the activity. No one is there to flaunt their figures or eye up others. Instead, people of all shapes and sizes sit side by side for the same purpose: to cleanse the body and soul and to relax. Just don't forget to bring a small towel to sit on!

Reasons to *bada bastu*

The positive effects of taking a sauna are well documented. While the heat helps to flush away impurities, leaving you with a glowing complexion, the hot–cold treatment helps relieve stress, improve circulation, boost immunity and relieve pain. In fact, a recent study by the University of Eastern Finland even found that frequent sauna use is good for your heart![10]

So why not find a sauna in your area? Your mind and body will thank you for it. If the idea of going in the buff makes you feel a little hot under the collar, rest assured that in the UK it's standard to wear a bathing suit or cover your dangly bits with a strategically placed towel – phew!

Sauna etiquette

+ Take a small towel to sit on.

+ Leave your clothes and bathing suit at the door (unless it's mixed sex or you're in the UK).

+ Keep your voice low.

+ Make room for others as they enter.

+ Check with others before throwing water over the coals.

INTO THE WILD

Mention there's a forest down the road, and a Swede will be off faster than you can fill your Thermos. Sweden has 29 national parks and more than half of the country is covered in forest, so the countryside is a huge part of life. *Allemansrätten*, translated as 'everyman's right', gives people the right to roam freely and enjoy activities such as foraging for wild fruit and camping wherever they choose (as long as they're not disturbing others). As a result, it's not unusual for Swedes to take a picnic and enjoy an outdoor adventure no matter the weather – with activities ranging from hiking to sailing, kayaking, cross-country skiing and even dog-sledding.

I'm convinced these activities contribute to the Swedes' inner calm, and there are an increasing number of studies showing nature's significant positive effects. A 2016 campaign by The Wildlife Trusts found people who regularly engaged in activities connected to nature showed a significant increase in happiness and health.[11] Other research has also shown nature to soothe, heal and help restore our minds, as well as boost creativity. The next time you're feeling the heat, why not pack a picnic and head outdoors?

'There is a pleasure in the pathless woods, There is a rapture on the lonely shore, There is a society where none intrudes, By the deep sea, and music in its roar: I love not Man the less, but Nature more.'

Lord Byron, *Childe Harold*, Canto IV, Verse 178

Five ways to enjoy
the great outdoors

Smultronställe (n.): lit. 'Place of wild strawberries'
A special place discovered, treasured, returned to for solace
and relaxation; a personal idyll free from stress or sadness.

Pack a picnic and head to your nearest wood or forest (even if it rains, you'll have a natural canopy overhead).

Break out the wellies for an afternoon and go foraging for berries, herbs or mushrooms. You'll be amazed by what you can find (though be sure to check with an expert to see if what you've found is edible).

Take a stroll along a beach and enjoy shell-seeking or casting stones into the water. A Thermos of coffee and a blanket will keep you warm while you stop and gaze at the horizon.

Rent a kayak or stand-up paddle (SUP) and head to a nearby river, lake or shoreline.

If you live near the sea, put your name forward to crew at a local sailing club. A patient skipper will appreciate the extra deckhand and be happy to show you the ropes.

Dare to go alone

My Swedish friend Yvonne recounted how she'd once gone on a solitary five-day hike across a nature reserve. Although she confessed that 'it's incredible just how many noises there are in the woods at night', the only time she was uncomfortable was when a party set up camp next to her and played the guitar until the small hours. Above all else, she enthused about how liberating and empowering the experience was.

To be honest with you, I can't quite see myself camping alone in the woods at night, but it does inspire me to head out for a few hours to feel the power of being alone in nature, and I hope it does the same for you. It's in these solitary moments that you appreciate the rustle of the leaves in the wind, the sound of the breaking waves or the distant melody of a lark. The unbroken spell of nature allows you to slow down, switch off and be alone with your thoughts – something of a rarity in the noisy world in which we live today.

Whistle while you walk

If you do head out to a forest alone, be careful to whistle, stamp your feet and generally make some noise – bears and wolves are shy but hate being caught off guard!

A beginner's guide to foraging

If you go to the Swedish woods in late summer/early autumn, you'll come across people armed with baskets, scouring the forest floor for edible mushrooms, berries and other delicacies. Foraging is a skill that requires knowledge, patience and an eager eye, but once you get the hang of it, it's great fun and incredibly mindful. And it makes for a tasty supper, too! It's amazing what you can find at your feet if you just open your eyes. Here's how to get started:

+ **Find out more about the foliage in your area:** identify the different species of weed, bush or tree. Learn what's in season and at what point it should be harvested, and check it's not on the endangered-species list.

+ **Identify poisonous plants** and never, ever eat anything you're not 150 per cent sure about: always check your wares, preferably with an expert.

+ **Gather only what you need** and avoid taking everything from the patch; it's also important to give the area time to recover before you return.

+ **Avoid polluted areas,** whether it's the roadside or places where crops have been treated by chemicals.

+ **Have fun:** edible wild food can be quite hard to find, but if you make a day of it and take a picnic, it'll be worth the effort.

Five edible mushrooms and where to find them*

+ **Chicken-of-the-woods –** *Laetiporus sulphureus* Once you know what you're looking for, you'll find this yellow-orange mushroom everywhere on the trunks and branches of living and felled trees.

+ **Lion's mane –** *Hericium erinaceus* This distinct and delectable mushroom can be found on dying or recently felled hardwood trees like maples, sycamores and oaks.

+ Chanterelle mushroom – *Cantharellus cibarlus* The chanterelle is a forager's favourite because it's delicious. You can find it almost everywhere in the world.

+ Cauliflower mushroom – *Sparassis* Usually found living in the roots or at the base of a hardwood tree, the cauliflower mushroom is best picked when white and is delicious served in an omelette.

+ Porcini mushroom – *Boletus edulis* Found on a hardwood forest floor near chestnuts, spruce, pine and hemlock, this mushroom has a nutty taste and is a real gourmet treat.

*Mushrooms can be deadly poisonous, so always consult an expert before consuming.

HOLIDAYS

If you visit Sweden in June, you'll feel a buzz of excitement
in the air. The warm weather will have arrived and people
all over the country are preparing to shut their laptops and
shut up shop for the summer. Some may stay put and enjoy
some downtime in their own back garden; others will visit
a basic summer cottage by the water's edge or go camping.
Either way, the goal is the same: to take time off to enjoy
the simple things in life – long hours of daylight, nature and
being together with friends and family.

The basic summer cottage

Living in Sweden has reconfirmed my belief that you don't have to spend a lot to have a magical holiday. The Swedish summer holiday is about taking time out and going back to basics to enjoy the simple things in life – whether that's simply hanging out at home or heading to a small, basic summer cottage by the sea or deep in the heart of the countryside, to enjoy reading, baking, bathing, board games, crafting or simply hanging out with friends and family and drinking in as much sunlight as possible before the autumn leaves start to fall.

In a fast-paced digital world, taking time just to 'be' is the perfect antidote. Expectations are minimized – it's a fuss-free adventure without a large investment, and there's no pressure: no flights to catch, no currencies to decipher or schedules to stick to. The time is simply there for you to enjoy in whichever way you choose.

The next time you're booking your vacation, I can highly recommend finding a small cottage or cabin not far from home. It doesn't have to be grand – in fact, the smaller and more basic the better. It only needs to be somewhere you can switch off and chill out – no Pokémon GO in sight!

<u>Camping</u>

Camping is the perfect way to enjoy a slower-paced life and the freedom that comes from enjoying the vastness of nature, without keys or a credit card in your pocket. Head out to the countryside, find a secluded spot and soak up the fresh air and peaceful environment. Not much of a Boy Scout/Girl Guide? Find a 'glamp' site near you for camping with a touch of comfort, like a proper bed and a hot-water bottle. You'll still find the odd spider, though!

Five ways to enjoy camping

Have all the gear and some idea!
Make sure you're properly equipped
with everything you need and test it
in the garden (or in your sitting room!)
before you set off. That way you
won't forget vital items, such as the
tent poles (been there, done that!).
Likewise, pack suitable clothing for all
conditions, a first-aid kit and that all-
important mosquito repellent!

Find an incredible setting The
beauty of camping is that you can
decide on the view! Set aside some
time to research great camping
spots before you head off and then
choose the perfect place to pitch
your tent on arrival, ensuring it's flat,
with good drainage, and has the most
stunning view!

**Make the most of what nature has
to offer** Embrace the simple things
in life and enjoy swimming in a lake
or the sea, hiking, or just taking in the
scenery, followed by an evening under
the stars!

Ensure a good night's sleep Unless
you're Bear Grylls, you'll appreciate
some home comforts. Pack an
inflatable or foam mattress, your pillow
and even some ear plugs and an eye
mask – and wake up rested and raring
to go!

Treat yourself You may love baked
beans – in which case, great! But if
you prefer something a little more
gourmet, there are many fantastic
one-pot recipes out there – and
don't forget the hot chocolate and
marshmallows!

The lagom guide to physical happiness

We can't all be naturally blessed with a flowing mane of golden hair and a lithe physique, but we can learn a thing or two from Swedes about how to look after our bodies. They take a no-nonsense approach, simply enjoying a balanced diet, neither denying themselves that cinnamon bun nor overdoing the salad. They also naturally incorporate exercise into their day, favouring the bike over a car or public transport, whether there's sun, rain, wind or snow. So even on the busiest of days, they've got their heart pumping.

EATING IN MODERATION

It's safe to say that if you're not a fan of fish or potatoes, you might struggle in Sweden. No holiday smorgasbord is complete without them. National dishes (or *husmanskost*) include *sill och potatis* (a serving of herring and potatoes with lingonberries), *köttbullar med potatismos* (meatballs and mash) and *pyttipanna* (a mix of cubed potatoes, meat and onion with a side of pickled beetroot). Joking aside, the Nordic diet is fast being recognized for its health benefits. The average life expectancy in Sweden is 80.3 years for men and 84.1 years for women, which puts the country firmly in the top ten of the World Health Organization's ranking system.

Nordic meals are all about balance and eating seasonal produce. In fact, a study by the Nordic Centre of Excellence demonstrated that a healthy Nordic diet can improve cholesterol levels, lower the risk of coronary heart disease and reduce inflammatory conditions (such as arthritis and Crohn's disease).[12] In other words, it's good for your heart and waistline!

Eat the Swedish way

Herring: Salted, smoked, fried or pickled, there's evidence to suggest the humble herring has been on the Nordic menu since Neolithic times. This small fish is relatively cheap to buy and easy to store. It's a great source of vitamin D and is rich in omega-3 fatty acids, which are known to prevent heart disease, help your brain function and boost your immune system.

Potatoes: A staple around the world, the common spud carries many health benefits. The vegetable is rich in potassium (helping to lower blood pressure), fibre and vitamins C and B. Once cooked, it's high in resistant starch, which ultimately helps the body burn fat.

Filmjölk: A traditional fermented milk, this healthy dairy product is commonly eaten with cereal at breakfast time. The lactic acid bacteria 'is considered to facilitate the digestive process, strengthen the immune system and reduce the risk of allergy', explains Richard Löfgren, from dairy company Skånemejerier.

Lingonberry: Also known as cowberries, mountain cranberries and partridge berries, lingonberries grow in Nordic forests and are enjoyed as jam, with pancakes or as a relish. Not only are they packed with antioxidants, vitamins A and C, fibres and magnesium, researchers at Lund University[13] have found that they can also help regulate your metabolism.

Crispbread: Known locally as *knäckebröd*, crispbread has been a staple in the Swedish diet since AD 500. In part, its popularity is thanks to its long expiry date and low price, but it's also been found to have health benefits. Traditionally made from wholemeal rye flour, salt and water, it's low in fat, high in fibre and packed with vitamins, antioxidants and minerals.

Rotten fish

Although Swedes have mastered the art of moderation, there's one thing that even they agree is far from lagom: *surströmming*. Famous for its overwhelmingly putrid smell and strong, acidic taste, it's herring treated with just the right amount of salt to prevent it from going rotten. Then it's left to go off for just over six months before it's tinned. The fermented herring is served once a year (somewhere around the third Thursday in August) and consumed outdoors – preferably while holding your nose.

EXERCISE

You may be someone who loves to work up a sweat at the gym or take a 10k run before breakfast. If so, great! But in our increasingly busy lives, it can be hard to find time to fit in a workout. Fear not, though – I've noticed that, as part of the lagom mind-set, Swedes are adept at incorporating exercise into their daily lives without breaking into a sweat. Experts also agree that by making small changes to your daily life (such as cycling or walking instead of driving), you can enjoy benefits such as a reduced risk of coronary disease, lower blood pressure, weight loss and lower stress levels.

Five easy ways to integrate exercise into your daily life

Cycle or walk to work. Research has linked walking or cycling to work with improved mental well-being.[14] In other words, ditching the daily car ride for a physical mode of transport makes you happier. Hurrah!

Park at the back of the car park or get off the train one stop early and then walk the extra distance. It may not seem like much but these extra steps build up over time.

Take the stairs instead of the lift. It's said you burn approximately 0.17 calories for every step you climb, which equates to 1.5 calories every ten steps! Reason enough to skip the lift and climb the stairs instead?

Stand rather than sit at your desk. Did you know that a 150lb person burns 114 calories an hour simply from standing? That's 912 calories a day. Time to take a stand!

Walk and talk. Skip the café and get a latte-to-go instead. Meeting up with friends provides the perfect opportunity to take a leisurely walk in nice surroundings and catch up at the same time.

Pedal power

Making the move from London to Malmö was something of a culture shock. And, believe it or not, one of the biggest shocks of all was swapping the London Underground for the bicycle lanes of Malmö. Now, Malmö is a great city for cyclists: it's relatively small and flat and has a myriad of cycle paths, complete with traffic lights, priority crossings and pump stations. In fact, it was recently ranked sixth in The Copenhagenize Bicycle Friendly Cities Index (http://copenhagenize.eu/index). But what I struggled with is that, in Sweden, cycling is an integral part of daily life – going to the supermarket, collecting the kids from school, nipping into town or even going to the pub. Pedal power is the transport of choice, rain, snow or shine!

I've adapted over time, and today I think nothing of using my bike daily. In fact, I find it a lot more practical and can highly recommend it. With more than a billion people worldwide getting into cycling and roads becoming more bike friendly, here are nine great reasons you should think about hopping on your bike, too:

+ You will save money on fuel

+ You will save time waiting for public transport

+ There's no need to look for a parking space

+ You can avoid traffic jams

+ It can be enjoyed by all ages

+ You get fresh air

+ It's better for the environment

+ It's great for your health

+ It's a good stress buster

DRESSING FOR THE WEATHER

Fashionistas, look away now – when it comes to dressing the lagom way, it's all about being practical. Whether we're talking about a quick trip to the local shop, everyday work attire, a night out on the town or coping with extreme weather, the Swedes know how to get their clothing just right!

Style the simple way

Spend a morning people-watching from a café and you'll see that Swedes tend to go for a more minimalist style of dress. Clothes are characterized by clean lines and simple colour blocks, with a hint of the latest trends. It's highly practical, because most things are easy to mix and match, which not only saves time in the morning but also means each item goes that bit further.

The capsule wardrobe

Loosely speaking, the Swedish wardrobe could be likened to a capsule wardrobe – a minimalist, highly practical closet, created by clearing out unwanted or unused clothes and replacing them with a limited number of loved, highly versatile garments, which can ultimately be worn together.

Because a capsule wardrobe makes it easy to pick an outfit, you take the stress out of getting dressed and spend less time and energy on shopping and laundry. It's also more economical, and those who try it say it makes them feel happier.

'As I started living with a small, intentional wardrobe, I noticed that I felt joyful again,' enthuses Caroline Rector, founder of blog Un-Fancy.com. 'I saw, with fresh eyes, that happiness, contentment and joy come from within – not from stuff or external circumstances.' Really, what's not to love?

Six steps to creating
a capsule wardrobe

Remove every single item from your wardrobe and lay everything out in front of you.

Separate the garments into four piles: items you love and wear now, pieces you never wear but have kept for sentimental reasons, garments you no longer wear and dislike, and pieces that belong to another season. Store out-of-season garments and other pieces you can't bear to part with, and either sell or donate clothes you no longer wear.

Arrange the remaining items into a series of outfits. Each and every piece should mix and match with two or more other outfits.

Narrow the selection down to anywhere between 20 and 40 items (depending on your different needs, that is, if you have a separate work style, you may need more pieces). This includes tops, bottoms, dresses, outerwear and shoes, but not accessories like hats, scarves and jewellery. If necessary, shop for anything missing in your collection.

Neatly store away out-of-season items and arrange this season's garments in your wardrobe so that everything is clearly visible. Stick to the season's items for three months (in other words, a season without shopping – gasp!).

Make a plan for your next capsule wardrobe two weeks before the next season. Pull out next season's garments from storage and lay them out alongside the items in your wardrobe. Make a note of any items you are missing, keeping new purchases to a minimum.

A lagom guide to keeping warm and dry

When I first moved to Sweden, I can't tell you how many times I cycled to a meeting and arrived looking like a drowned rat, or wore white trousers to nursery parties (how was I to know we were going to eat barbecued hotdogs while sitting on the forest floor?). But eventually these wardrobe malfunctions wore me down, and I slowly adapted.

These days I wear practical, weather-appropriate clothes that keep me dry and comfortable, no matter what the temperature. And guess what? I feel far happier and more relaxed for it. Don't get me wrong, there's a time and place for the little black dress – it's just that there's also a time for long johns and waterproof trousers (and in the north, even a thermal skirt – yes, really!).

From footwear to foot-aware

'There is no such thing as bad weather, only bad clothing.'
Swedish proverb

꙾

If you've ever tried to navigate the cobbles of a Swedish square
or cycled into town in high heels, you'll know where I'm heading
with this. As with most things Swedish, the emphasis for footwear
is on practicality and comfort. The lagom shoe is not too flat, not
too high, waterproof, breathable and increasingly sustainable.

You still see kitten heels, but they're mainly confined to
bars and nightclubs. 'My shoes need to conform to my lifestyle
and ensure I'm ready for anything – like running straight from
a business meeting to the school gates,' Elin Sigrén, the stylish
Swedish jewellery designer and founder and CEO of SÄGEN,
tells me.

She has a point. Not only are flat shoes practical but
they're also better for our health. Countless studies have
shown that prolonged use of heels can lead to a dozen injuries,
including weak ankle muscles, shortening of the Achilles
tendon and back pain. Trust me, the lagom shoe is in, and
your body will thank you for it.

The effortless hair

Of course, many Swedes are lucky enough to be blessed with a beautiful blonde mane, but it's how they wear it that fascinates me. Loose, scraped back into a ponytail or pinned up – it doesn't matter as long as it gets you out of the door quickly! Needless to say, it will still look effortlessly cool.

Take the just-got-out-of-bed bun, also known as a topknot. So simple, so quick – and you can update it in the evening with a twist or plait for the ultimate Swedish hairstyle. But as 'thrown together' as it may appear, there is a strategy involved.

How to achieve the messy top knot

+ Ensure your hair isn't newly washed (it's far trickier to achieve this style with silky smooth hair).

+ Scrape your hair together and pull it straight up over your head.

+ Twist it downwards towards the crown, stopping an inch above your head.

+ Wrap the hair around itself to form a loose bun.

+ Use as many kirby grips or bobby pins as you need for a secure hold.

+ Tease out a few strands to give it that 'I've worn this bun all day and night' look, and *varsågod* ('there you go').

The lagom key
to success

Most people equate success with a high-flying career and a million in the bank. I would have done the same before moving to Sweden. Perhaps the most liberating lesson of all has been feeling satisfied with 'enough'. If you have the expectation that having more is equal to happiness, you'll always be left wanting. By building a life around less material items, you'll feel less pressure and stress and find the freedom to focus on more important things, such as spending time with family and friends and doing the things you love.

WORK–LIFE BALANCE

Having worked in Dubai, London, Copenhagen and Malmö, you could say I've experienced my fair share of work cultures. While each was as diverse as the last, there are a few key things separating Scandinavians from the rest.

In London, I found tiptoeing out of the office bang on time was considered 'clock watching' and was met with remarks like, 'Half-day today, Niki?' I was amazed (and somewhat grateful) to find that the moment the working day finishes in Scandinavia, people swarm out in lines with a cheery wave and a 'Have a nice evening!' In fact, I'd go a step further and say that working late is met with general concern. Managers start to question whether you've been given a burdensome workload, and a series of meetings might ensue.

Don't get me wrong – Swedes aren't sitting at work all day looking at the clock and willing it to be home time. On the contrary, I've noticed that people are incredibly hard-working and extremely focused. After all, Sweden is home to some of the most innovative companies in the world, including Tetra Pak, IKEA, Spotify and Skype. It's just that people here put their family and home life first. There may be a child waiting to be collected from nursery, a squash partner warming up on the courts or simply a fridge to be filled.

This culture means you're not waiting around for the boss to leave (I'm embarrassed to admit my team and I did this daily in London). It means you get to spend more valuable time with family and friends, doing the things you enjoy.

Moreover, it allows time for errands and other everyday chores, which makes you feel more organized, less stressed and ultimately happier.

A 2014 Gallup poll in the US showed that one in five employees working full time clocked up more than 60 hours a week. But these guys are missing a trick. A recent study showed productivity dramatically drops off after 50 hours a week, and that not taking a rest day (Sunday, for instance) leads to a lower hourly output.[15] In other words, reducing your working hours can boost productivity. Time to look to the Swedes for a more lagom way of working?

Be an early bird

I've never been a morning person, and chances are you're not either. Researchers from RWTH Aachen University in Germany found that only 10 per cent of us are early risers (compared to the 20 per cent of us who are night owls).[16] Not in Sweden. You can imagine my horror when I realized the country I now call home is a nation of early birds.

Although it may vary, the general working day starts at 8 a.m., with school commencing 8:15. Nightmare! But, once I got over the shock, the results surprised me. Not only have I found I'm way more productive in the mornings but I'm more creative, too.

The Swedes (and I) are not alone. Apple CEO Tim Cook famously wakes up at an eye-watering 3:45 a.m. to get a head start on emails. Michelle Obama begins her daily workout at 4:30 a.m., and former Xerox CEO Ursula Burns rises at 5:15 a.m. Interestingly, a study by biologist Christopher Randler revealed that early risers are more proactive.[17] Using the early hours to plan and anticipate problems boosts productivity and, ultimately, success. Time to reset that alarm clock!

Four reasons to become an early riser

+ **Fewer distractions:** With fewer people around, you're more likely to find that 'me time' to read the newspaper or get started on emails.

+ **Time to exercise:** The first few hours of the day might be the only time you can find to exercise. Give yourself an early-morning energy boost and you'll be more productive afterwards.

+ **Time for breakfast:** It's considered the most important meal of the day, and rising with the lark gives you time to start off in a healthier way.

+ **You'll be happier:** Yes, really! According to a study by the University of Toronto,[18] people who rise early are happier than night owls.

How to trick yourself into being an early riser

These reasons are all well and good, but what if (like me) you're not a morning person?

Visualize Before you go to sleep, take time to imagine the sacred hour you'll have before the rest of the world awakes. Sipping a slow-brewed coffee. Strolling along the beach. Silence!

Let the sun shine in The moment you wake up, pull back the curtains to allow daylight to flood the room (unless it's deep mid winter and you're living in Sweden, in which case best just to turn on a light). Or go a step further: open your windows and inhale the fresh morning air.

Enjoy your morning You earned these hours, so make sure you do the things that make you happy. You'll be much more likely to repeat the ritual if you associate getting up early with positive memories.

Be kind Invest in an alarm clock that simulates sunrise. In winter this allows light to enter your sphere slowly.

Get tough More often than not, actually getting out of bed is the hard part. If none of the above is working, try placing your alarm clock several metres away (or in another room) so you have to get up to switch it off.

TAKE A BREAK

Step inside a Swedish workplace and the first thing you'll notice is how quiet it is. Everyone is beavering away and there's no persistent hum of idle chatter. Of course, you'll be greeted with a cheery wave when you arrive, and there may be the odd huddle of people talking in hushed voices. But chances are it's strictly work-related. You see, in Swedish offices, most social chitchat is reserved for breaks.

Taking time out

The Swedish *fikapaus* is a break with a coffee and maybe a little treat. It could be an informal catch-up with a colleague prompted by a simple, 'Shall we have a coffee at 10? I'd really like to hear about your holiday/weekend/nightmare neighbour.' Or it could be a more formal team *fika*, scheduled in the calendar months before. Formal or informal, it's about taking time to switch off for a few minutes and giving yourself a breather.

Speaking as someone who took some time to get used to this idea, you may feel a twinge of guilt at the self-indulgence. But, actually, putting your feet up once in a while makes total personal and business sense.

A study by psychological scientists Emily Hunter and Cindy Wu at Baylor University's Hankamer School of Business[19] found that people who took morning breaks at work reported feeling more energized, more able to concentrate and more motivated, and were less likely to report symptoms like

headaches and lower back pain. Interestingly, though, these positive effects fell the more time that elapsed between each break. In other words, taking short, regular breaks is key!

How to get into the habit

+ **The 52–17-minute rule:** A recent study found that the most productive people work for 52 minutes and then take a 17-minute break.[20] Of course, not all jobs allow for this, but it's worth thinking about the frequency – and keeping it in mind!

+ **Set a reminder:** It sounds geeky, but a formal reminder to take a breather could be what you need. A study conducted by Cornell University at the Wall Street office of New Century Global found that people who were sent a reminder to take a short break and think about their posture were, on average, 13 per cent more accurate than co-workers.[21]

+ **Note to introverts:** If the thought of making small talk can sometimes feel exhausting, there's nothing wrong with sloping off and indulging in some much-needed time alone – whether it's taking a walk around the block, quietly sipping a coffee or doing whatever you need to do to feel rested. I learnt this from the global HR director at my former company here in Sweden. He announced that, as an introvert, this was exactly how he was planning to spend his break, and that we should follow suit if desired. Music to every introvert's ears!

YOU DON'T HAVE TIME
TO SKIP LUNCH

In London, I was used to grabbing a sandwich at a nearby deli and taking it back to my desk. And I wasn't alone. A 2012 Right Management survey found that only one in five Americans took a lunch break, and a 2014 British Bupa survey discovered that only a third of British employees leave their desks for lunch.

Not in Sweden. Lunch is taken incredibly seriously. It's very rare to see Swedes tucking into meatballs and mash at their desk. First, it's eaten in a restaurant of some sort. Second, it's usually warm and fairly substantial. Third, they take their time. Taking a proper lunch break has been found to have numerous positive effects, including boosting productivity, creativity, energy, concentration and alertness in the afternoon. Plus, it helps you connect with the people around you.

You are
what you eat

We all know that what we eat for lunch affects our waistline, but did you know it can also contribute to how much energy we have in the afternoon?

Five brain-boosting foods

+ Raw vegetables

+ Nuts and seeds

+ Fish

+ Avocado

+ Dark chocolate (oh yes!)

'One cannot think well,
love well, sleep well, if
one has not dined well.'

Virgina Woolf,
A Room of One's Own

Five great things to
do at lunchtime

In our busy lives, time is a precious resource – and we should be mindful about how we use it. The lunch break is no different. Depending on your contract, it's 30–60 minutes of free time, and if we're to embrace the Swedish ethos of taking a decent break, there's usually a little time left after eating to spend exactly as you please. Use it wisely, and you'll not only enhance your well-being; you'll boost your career, too!

Arrange a date Invite a colleague you'd like to get to know better or an old friend who works near by and chat to your hearts' content about life, love and everything in between.

Get your blood pumping Go for a power walk or jog, or attend a lunchtime gym class. It will re-energize you in time for the afternoon shift.

Don your headphones and rock out to your favourite tunes Listening to music lights up your entire brain and is said to make you happier, smarter and more productive.[22]

Indulge in the arts Visit a nearby gallery or museum, learn photography via an app on your phone or simply read a book – and allow your mind to switch off from work.

Meditate Find a quiet spot to practise meditation. It will help relieve symptoms of stress and de-clutter your brain, preparing your mind, body and soul for the afternoon.

Revive your workspace

Your environment can also have a significant effect on your well-being and productivity. If you work from home or have your own office, you're lucky enough to have complete control. But there are small updates you can make in an office, too:

+ **Fight for the window seat:** Swedish architects are famous for drawing natural light into buildings, and there's good reason for this. A study by the Neuroscience Programme at Northwestern University in Chicago found a strong relationship between exposure to daylight at work and sleep quality, performance and general quality of life.[23]

+ **Temperature:** In Sweden, interiors are so well insulated that my mother complains she can't hear the birds singing. But it's actually extremely practical. If you're left shivering or baking hot, your energy is spent regulating your body temperature instead of focusing on the task at hand. Research suggests setting the thermostat at a surprisingly balmy 22–25°C (71.6–77°F) to ensure maximum comfort and work performance.[24]

+ **Get comfy:** Admittedly, I'm a little old fashioned, and I was a bit grumpy when an ergonomic specialist came to our office in Lund to check we were sitting correctly. A few weeks later, a ream of office equipment arrived – including footstools, swivel chairs and wrist supports. I was vastly more comfortable, and I conceded that perhaps my Swedish employer was ahead of the game. I've since learnt that ergonomically designed furniture can reduce issues like lower back pain, improve office morale and boost productivity!

+ **Take a stand:** From the moment I stepped on to Scandinavian soil, I've enjoyed an electric height-adjustable desk. It's quite fun, and it seems there are tremendous health benefits, too. American physician Dr David Angus famously asserted that sitting at your desk for five or more hours a day is the equivalent to smoking over a packet of cigarettes a day (eeek!). So if you have a job that involves lots of sitting, make sure you stand up once in a while.

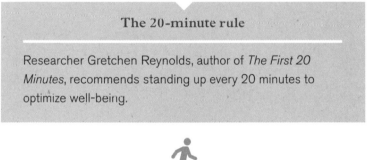

The 20-minute rule

Researcher Gretchen Reynolds, author of *The First 20 Minutes*, recommends standing up every 20 minutes to optimize well-being.

<u>Go green</u>

On my first day at work in Sweden, my desk was empty except for a plant (even my computer hadn't arrived). And there was a good reason. As we've already covered (see pages 30–31), plants are said to improve air quality, concentration and workplace satisfaction. So much so that a recent study found greenery helped boost productivity by up to 15 per cent![25]

THE LAGOM GUIDE TO SWITCHING OFF AND SAVING UP

The internet is, of course, miraculous. I'll never forget showing it to my 95-year-old grandfather, who was astounded that we have the world at our fingertips 24 hours a day, seven days a week. With it, however, comes the expectation and pressure of being constantly available.

Imagine the freedom of being able to switch off from the constant stream of work calls and emails? Giving yourself the freedom to enjoy uninterrupted evenings with your family and friends or care-free holidays in the sun?

On the whole, Swedes are not only skilled at indulging in the odd face-to-face 'after work' (in moderation, of course) but they're also pros at taking downtime without fear of interruption and have a natural flair for conscious buying to ease financial pressure. Step this way!

After work, Swedish style

Skiers might be familiar with the term après ski. If you work in Sweden, you'll also be familiar with the phrase 'after work' or even *AW* (pronounced 'aah-v'). In London, after-work drinks are a spontaneous affair usually preceded by 'Fancy a quick pint?' (which we knew would not be quick). The Swedish *AW* often comes with a formal calendar invite months before the intended event. Of course, there are advantages and disadvantages to this, depending on how much you love a cheeky mid-week drink. Although I remain in the London camp, I've learnt that having fewer but more organized after-work drinks definitely has a positive side. Most importantly, your family aren't waiting for you while you take your (ahem) 'quick' detour on the way home. And if the event is planned in advance, more people from the office attend, which is a great way to expand your network and improve morale.

Disconnect

Before the age of mobile phones and the internet, you could leave work behind you and not think about it again until the next day. What a relaxing thought! These days, phones are buzzing with a constant stream of emails and meeting invites. Push mail is particularly distracting, and for many of us a temptation we simply can't resist. We might feel we're keeping on top of things and looking dedicated, but research has shown that this is having quite the opposite effect. A study by Future Work Centre in London found that leaving email on all day (including checking emails last thing at night and first thing in the morning) is triggering stress and negatively affecting home life. And this, in turn, has a negative effect on work performance. Who knew?

Four ways to switch off in the evening

+ Set a curfew.
+ Turn off push mail.
+ Turn on your out-of-office or, if needed, find a replacement in the hours you'll be unavailable.
+ Charge your phone in a remote part of the house.

ANNUAL LEAVE
LIKE A SWEDE

If there's something that Swedes take seriously, it's annual leave. Anyone who works with a client or subsidiary in Sweden will know that not much happens in the month of July. Why? Swedes have been battling through a long, dark cold winter. When the warm weather arrives, they're going to enjoy it! No guilt, no worries about what colleagues or clients are going to think; they're entitled to undisturbed time off. The norm is three to four weeks, and the focus is on unwinding and enjoying the simple life with family and friends.

Of course, work regulations don't allow everyone around the world to take four consecutive weeks off, but research has shown that many people aren't even taking all their allotted days. The Glassdoor-Harris Interactive Survey[26] found that one in four Americans don't use all their allocated paid vacation days, and, out of those, 61 per cent worked while on holiday. This is a crying shame when you look at the benefits of time off, including reduced stress, more energy, improved creativity, more productivity when you return to work – and having time to bond with your family. Not to mention the pure enjoyment of a piña colada at sunset.

The magic vacation number

A study led by a research team at the University of Tampere in Finland discovered that holiday happiness and satisfaction peaked after eight days on vacation.[27] It looks like it's the 14-day break rather than the seven-day one, then!

CONSCIOUS BUYING

'He who buys what he does not need steals from himself.'
Swedish proverb

~~~

When I first arrived in Sweden, I'd wander around the supermarket, picking items off the shelves. My Swedish husband would be one step behind, plucking items out of the basket and replacing them with more economical versions. Tight? Maybe. Wise? Definitely! I learnt that lagom spending is about budgeting and conscious buying, ensuring you allocate money to cover your basic needs and purchasing items that matter to you.

Saving for a rainy day

Experts tout many positive reasons to save money, including being able to afford things like a home, car or holiday, becoming financially independent and being prepared for unforeseen expenses or emergencies. Ultimately, putting money aside for a rainy day will make you feel less stressed, more in control of your finances and all-round happier. Now that's worth saving for!

How to save money
like a Swede

Jot down your purchases over a month to get an overview of where your money is going and analyse each expenditure to see if it's something you can cut back on – such as a mobile-phone service you don't use or a takeaway latte each morning. Small savings each day will free up money to pay off debts or help you save for things that give you greater pleasure, both now and in the future.

Clear out unwanted stuff, hold a garage (yard) sale, or participate in a local flea market.

Sign up for customer-reward programmes and use coupons and promotion codes.

Write down everything you spend in a month to keep track on where your money is going.

Make your own gifts for friends and family, instead of buying them.

Invite friends over rather than meeting in town and enjoy a cosy night at home.

Use your local library for books, music, films and other items available to loan.

Invest in quality appliances and furniture that will stand the test of time.

Bake your own bread (and freeze it for weekdays).

Cycle or walk instead of taking the car or public transport.

Organize a car share (carpool) system with people who share your journey.

Get digital

There is an increasing number of smartphone apps that can help you save money. Digit, for example, takes smaller or larger amounts from your bank account depending on how much money you have in your account at the time. Download a money-saving app that works for you and you could be travelling around the world before you know it!

02

Lagom in family and relationships

The lagom guide
to friendship

The respect for personal space in Sweden is mesmerizing (and at first a little baffling). When it comes to friendship, Swedes are wary about coming on too strong. It therefore takes a long time to form a friendship, but when you do, it's a bond that lasts a lifetime. Rather than rushing in, perhaps we can all learn to slow down, take our time to get to know people and truly listen to what they have to say. And who knows? We might find new friends in the most unexpected places!

'When you talk,
you are only repeating
what you already know.
But if you listen, you may
learn something new.'

Dalai Lama

THE ART OF LISTENING

Converse with a Swede and you'll notice that they very rarely interrupt or talk over anyone else. Voices are kept to even tones (unless there's schnapps involved), and pauses in conversation are completely acceptable. To Brits, this can feel excruciatingly awkward. Culturally, we're so concerned about a gap in the conversation that we constantly overlap before people have completed their sentence. Swedes feel slightly awkward in these silent moments, too, but rather than desperately fill the gap with a hurried slew of off-the-cuff words, they'll make sounds, like a sharp intake of breath or even a sing-song sound like a two-toned 'hmmm'. This gives them time to reflect on something meaningful that they can contribute.

This type of discourse doesn't work so well at a cocktail party where small talk abounds, but it will add more meaning to a full conversation. And, like all things lagom, it's a fairer, more equal conversation where everyone gets a chance to say something, rather than just the loudest person in the room.

The next time you're in a social situation or enjoying a break at work, I challenge you to give it a go. Slow down the discourse. Really listen to others and reflect on what they have to say. Once someone's finished speaking, take time to reflect (if needed) before giving a meaningful response. Once you get into the slower rhythm, you'll find it's so much more relaxing to speak without fear of interruption. And you might just learn some new, fascinating things about the person you're speaking to!

Being honest

Swede's call it being 'honest', my English friends call it being 'direct' – either way, you'll only ever hear the truth from a Swede. There's a saying in Swedish: 'Rather an honest "no" than an insincere "yes".'

Say a Swede notices your new haircut. They'd never say they like it when they don't, although they'd be way too polite to come out and say they don't like it unless they know you extremely well. Instead, they'd be silent. This lagom way of being honest (but not overly honest) means you can fully trust a Swede. And although it may hurt, you won't be walking around with a disastrous haircut for months. Something to think about the next time a friend asks for your opinion …

'A friend is someone who knows the song in your heart and can sing it back to you when you have forgotten the words.'

Donna Roberts

Being punctual

I'm ashamed to admit that if there's one thing I'm known for, it's poor timekeeping. Acknowledging this doesn't make it acceptable, but I know I'm not alone. Whether going to work, school, the gym or a party, people in many parts of the world are turning up later than ever before. There is, however, an exception: in Sweden. Organize a dinner party and you'll have guests lining up at your door before you've finished drying your hair.

But why? I turned to Sofia, my most punctual friend, for clarification. 'In Sweden people are used to everything working on time – buses, trains, doctor's appointments, etc. They therefore have the expectation that whoever they're meeting will be punctual,' she theorizes.

In a nation where respect is high on the agenda, punctuality is key. Although social norms vary from country to country, there are many positive incentives to be more punctual and show we care:

Six great reasons to turn up on time

+ It demonstrates respect and kindness towards others.
+ It shows you're trustworthy.
+ It makes you appear more diligent and professional.
+ It'll make you feel calmer and more organized.
+ You'll set a good example to your kids and others around you.
+ You'll keep the Swedes happy.

Undivided attention

Just how distracting is a mobile phone? It's sitting there in your pocket or lying on the table between you and your friend, beeping and buzzing away – begging you to look at it (chances are, it's just Sarah posting a picture of her lunch). And the moment your friend heads off to the bathroom, out it comes! Sadly, this has become the norm. However, today's social psychologists are advising people to consider leaving their mobile phone at home, or at least at the very bottom of their bag, so they can give their friends their undivided attention. I've noticed that in Sweden, although people do occasionally have their phones on the table, they will most likely have them on silent mode and face down as a mark of respect. We can all think more about being in the moment, though, and rather than whipping out our phones as soon as a friend goes up to refill their coffee, sit, relax and reflect on what's been said – or simply take in the atmosphere.

'Friendship isn't a big thing. It's a million little things.'

Anonymous

THE ART OF *FIKA*

Fika (fee-ka) (n): taking time for a coffee,
treats and conversation with friends.

~~~~~~

Fika is a sacred Swedish social ritual meaning 'taking a break for coffee and enjoying a small treat'. But it also means so much more than that. It's a moment to relax and *umgås* – 'hang out together' – and catch up with family and friends away from the stresses and strains of everyday life.

The beauty of *fika* is how uncomplicated it is. You can do it literally anywhere – at your kitchen table, at a local café, on the beach or even by the side of the road. And you can do it almost anytime – morning, noon, late afternoon or early evening (although strong coffee late at night is best avoided, even by Swedish standards!). All you need is a cup of coffee (or another hot drink) and, if you like, a small treat of some kind (one of the favourites being a cinnamon bun). The key is to stop whatever you're doing and take some time out to enjoy the simple, good things in life.

Fika lingo!

+ **Fikasugen** – a strong desire or craving for a *fika*
+ **Fikarum** – a designated room, where staff convene for coffee
+ **Fikapaus** – to stop what you're doing and enjoy a *fika*

Fika **for thought**

I'll never forget seeing two teenage girls in Denmark sitting on the beach, sharing a blanket and enjoying a coffee from a Thermos at sunset. The golden sunlight lit up their animated faces. The moment didn't cost a penny, but the enjoyment was palpable.

Coffee

Procaffeinating (n.): the tendency not to start anything until you've had a cup of coffee.

～～～

The first time I drank coffee in Sweden, I thought I'd been poisoned. I broke into a sweat, my palms felt itchy and my pulse was racing. It's real spoon-standing-up-in-the-cup stuff! In a country that ranks in the top three of global coffee consumers, Swedes slurp an average of three to five cups of coffee per day, sending their tolerance levels skywards – aided by the fact that in many cafés you also get the chance to *påtar* (refill free of charge).

Despite the negative publicity, you might be surprised to hear that drinking several cups of coffee a day can have positive side effects. Not only do coffee beans contain antioxidants and other nutrients but some studies have shown that multiple cups can also be good for your heart,[1] can help reduce the risk of multiple sclerosis by up to 30 per cent[2] and may even help protect against the recurrence of breast cancer.[3] Latte, anyone?

Swedish
treats

Having enjoyed many *fikas*, I can safely say that Swedes have
a very sweet tooth. *Dammsugare* (a punsch-liqueur flavoured
delicacy, covered in green marzipan and dipped in chocolate at
each end), *chokladbollar* (chocolate balls rolled in coconut) and
kanelbullar (cinnamon buns) are just a few *fika* staples. They're
of bite-sized proportions – just enough to satisfy that craving,
but not so big that you fall into a sugar-induced coma. In other
words, they're just right for a *fika*!

+ Chokladbollar

+ Kanelbullar

+ Dammsugare

+ Hallongrottan

+ Pepparkakor

+ Semla

GREAT-GRANDMOTHER OLGA JEPSSON'S
CINNAMON BUNS

▽

No *fika* is complete without the deliciously sweet Swedish *kanelbullar*, or cinnamon bun. It's so sacred it even has its own day (October 4). There are many variations, with each family having its own recipe going back generations. My husband's family is no different.

Makes approx. 10–12 buns

For the bun mixture
+ 450g (2 cups) good-quality plain flour, plus extra for dusting
+ 50g (¼ cup) caster or fine sugar
+ 25g (⅛ cup) dried yeast
+ ¼ tsp salt
+ 75g (⅓ cup) butter, cubed
+ 250ml (1 cup) warm milk

For the filling
+ 75g (⅓ cup) melted butter
+ 60g (⅓ cup) muscovado sugar or soft light brown sugar
+ 2–3 tbsp ground cinnamon (to taste)

To finish
+ 1 beaten egg, or milk, to glaze
+ pearl sugar, for sprinkling

1. Preheat the oven to 200°C/400°F/gas mark 6.

2. First, make the bun mixture. Combine the dry ingredients in a bowl and then mix in the butter, either using the dough hook attachment of your mixer or by rubbing it in with your fingertips, until it resembles damp sand.

3. Slowly add the warm milk while continuing to mix until it forms a dough. If the mixture appears sticky, add a small handful of flour.

4. Cover the bowl with a clean, dry tea towel and leave the dough to rise for an hour.

5. Transfer the dough to a floured surface and knead well for 5 minutes or until the dough is smooth and shiny. Roll out the dough to form an oblong shape approximately 1cm (just under ½ inch) thick.

6. For the filling, brush the surface with the melted butter, then sprinkle with the sugar and cinnamon.

7. Roll up the dough on the long side and cut into slices 3cm (about 1 inch) thick. Place the rolls cut-side up on a baking tray, spaced well apart. Cover with a tea towel and leave to rise for 45 minutes.

8. Brush with the beaten egg (or milk) and sprinkle with the pearl sugar, then bake in the preheated oven for 15 minutes or until the buns are golden brown, can be easily removed from the baking tray and sound hollow when tapped on the underside.

9. Remove from the oven and place on a cooling rack. Once cooled, eat immediately or store in an airtight container for 2–3 days. They are also suitable for home freezing (perfect for unexpected guests!).

HOW TO ENTERTAIN THE LAGOM WAY

Due to high taxes, eating and drinking out in Sweden has traditionally been costly. Although it's more affordable these days, Swedes will often suggest meeting at home rather than in town. Home entertainment is usually a fairly informal affair – the key is keeping it simple. I've been to some lovely dinner parties where the host has served a wonderful meal, but it's also not uncommon to suggest a get-together where everyone chips in with whatever they have in the fridge (even bringing their own cutlery, plates and tables if the numbers require it!). The result is a relaxed, fuss-free event where everyone has a lagom amount to do.

Four easy ways to spend time with friends

The next time you put off a get-together with friends because of time, energy or budget, how about suggesting one of the following ideas:

Picnics In warmer months, picnics are the ideal easy meal. They require little in the way of planning (everyone can grab whatever they have in the fridge) and preparation (no homes to tidy or big supermarket trips), they can be enjoyed anywhere (although I do love to sit by the water) and can be great fun, too. Just keep your fingers crossed that the weather holds up!

Barbecue Brush off the grill for a relaxed get-together in your back garden, out in the woods or on the beach. It's not about wowing people with butterflied king prawns or popping champagne corks (beer or a humble boxed wine is the preferred choice at Swedish barbecues). Rather, it's about keeping it hassle-free, with everyone bringing something to throw on the grill.

Waffle afternoon Forget high tea. In Sweden, if it's not a *fika*, it's all about the waffles. The beauty of them is that they're simple to make (pour homemade batter over a waffle iron), easy to serve (I like mine with strawberry jam and whipped cream) and popular among all ages, too!

Build a bonfire In spring, Swedes who live in apartments with communal gardens set aside a *städdag,* or a date to prepare the garden together for the outdoor season. Whether you have your own garden or shared outdoor space, why not gather friends and have fun raking up dead leaves, pruning the hedges and clearing away moss before throwing it on a bonfire? Long sticks are a perfect tool for heating sausages over an open flame – and don't forget the marshmallows!

Keep warm like a Swede

Wander around a Swedish city centre at night and you'll see people doggedly sitting outside restaurants and bars long after the sun's warmth has dwindled. Why? Fleece blankets are draped over the backs of chairs, ready to be used at the slightest sign of a chill. If you're having an outdoor gathering, prepare a basket of rolled-up blankets (they don't need to match) for when the temperature starts to drop. They're perfect for snuggling under, and it means the party can continue long after sunset!

The lagom guide
to relationships

It seems strange to begin a chapter about
relationships talking about independence, but I've
realized it's fundamental to understanding a Swedish
relationship. You see, independence is pivotal in
Swedish society. The entire system is designed so that
people can fend for themselves: heavily subsidized
day-care centres, for example, mean that once
parental leave is over everyone can and *is* expected
to work (unless physically or mentally incapable) and
contribute to household income. And, from there, a
truly balanced and healthy relationship is born.

FINDING BALANCE

I've learnt that taking equal responsibility
for all aspects of life plays an essential role in
Swedish relationships. Whether it's working,
dividing up household chores, childcare,
initiating sex or simply giving the other
person space to enjoy some all-important
me time – doing your bit is the key
to finding balance.

Being together – but not too together

Being a fairly liberal country, Sweden is known for its relaxed attitude towards sex and relationships (Sweden legalized same-sex marriage in 2009, the seventh country in the world to do so). And in a culture that highly values independence, it's perfectly acceptable to live together or apart and never get married. In fact, they've even devised words for these options. For example, *särbo* is used to describe your partner when you're in a relationship but live separately, and *sambo* is a partner you live with but aren't married to. It's not uncommon for couples to be together for 40 years or more and never get married.

Regardless of type, there is one vital factor that binds Swedish relationships, generally, and it ties in with the lagom philosophy: it's centred on kindness, respect and working together as a team – in all aspects!

Relationship equality

It's little wonder that Sweden is known for being the most progressive country in the world in terms of gender equality: it's something everyone in the country has strived for and feels immensely proud of, although they will tell you there's still more work to be done. I've learnt that it makes sense for both people in a relationship to take equal responsibility for income, household chores, raising the children and just about every other area in their joined lives. If these tasks are divided effectively and each partner trusts the other to get on with it, it leads to an even-handed relationship, in which everyone has a lagom amount to do and both can enjoy a balanced way of life. Hurrah!

1974

The year Sweden became the first country to replace maternity leave with parental leave.

480

The number of paid parental leave days in Sweden, which can be shared.

85%

The percentage of Swedish fathers who take parental leave.

Dividing up chores

A few years back, I found myself in a situation in which I needed to sew some fabric together (surprisingly rare!). I borrowed a sewing machine and tentatively got to work. A few minutes later my husband appeared, asked me what needed to be done and sat at the machine. Within a few minutes he had knocked out two beautiful cushion covers. I stood there astonished. 'We learnt at school,' he shrugged.

One of the key points here, though, is that from childhood Swedes are taught that household chores should be divided up according to preference, not gender. Someone who's a bit of a whizz at cooking and finds it relaxing, for example, might prefer to take on more in the kitchen. Others might love to wander around the supermarket or do the laundry (there must be someone out there who enjoys it!). And if no one raises their hand then you simply take turns.

Time to do what you love

Dividing up responsibilities with your partner is a great way to find more balance in your life and free up time for doing what you love – together and apart. In a nation where independence is cherished, creating time for and encouraging activities like meeting a friend, doing a project you're passionate about, going to the gym or taking up a new hobby separate from your other half is said to be key to maintaining a healthy and balanced lagom relationship.

Be kind

'Love me when I least deserve it,
because this is when I need it the most.'
Swedish proverb

Looking for the key to a long, happy relationship? Leading relationship experts say kindness and generosity towards one another is the secret.[4] As with all things lagom, they don't need to be grand gestures – small, thoughtful actions that don't require a lot of effort can often go a long way and put a smile on your loved one's face! My husband, for example, is always doing little things like bringing me coffee in bed in the morning, stocking the fridge with my favourite chocolate and sending thoughtful texts. Nothing grand, just simple things, which make my day that little bit brighter!

Five small things to do for your partner to show you care

+ Ask: 'Is there anything I can do for you today?'
+ Leave a personal note in the book they're reading to make them smile.
+ Surprise them with coffee or tea in bed on a regular day.
+ Pick up one of their favourite treats on your way home.
+ Mend their bicycle without being asked.

The lagom guide to sex

When it comes to the bedroom, Swedes are known for their liberal attitude. My Swedish husband still jokes about the time he came to my parents' house when we were both in our twenties, and we had to sleep in separate bedrooms! Parents in Sweden are, in general, much more relaxed, taking pains to talk to their children about safe sex and respecting that if something's going to happen, it's better that it happens under the safety of their roof (as long as they are of legal age) rather than behind their backs. How refreshing!

PLAN A WEDDING LIKE A SWEDE

Having moved to Sweden in my mid-twenties, our first few summers were a blur of hen and stag dos and weddings – on both sides of the North Sea.

While all were great fun and truly memorable in their own way, I observed that while English hen and stag dos tended to be slightly more lavish affairs (often involving flights and hotels), the Swedish equivalent was more about coming up with creative ways to have fun – often on your own doorstep. This extended to the big day itself, with Swedish weddings usually fairly relaxed affairs, where the guests do their fair share of making the day memorable (and I'm not just talking about going for it on the dance floor!).

All in all, in Sweden the big day is about finding a balance – ensuring that costs are kept down for all involved and the focus is on being together.

The Swedish hen and stag do

Forget Ibiza drink-fests or luxurious spa weekends. In Sweden, hen and stag dos are simply about creating a truly personal, memorable event and helping friends and relatives get to know each other before the big day. Traditionally, the maid of honour or best man organizes it without the bride or groom's knowledge (they're sprung upon in the morning). This means the bride and groom are in a state of nervous anticipation because they know a hen or stag do is inevitable but aren't quite sure when it will be! In the months before the wedding, the group gets together to plan a day (or occasionally a weekend) of activities, from a picnic to scavenger hunts and dance sessions or going out on a boat. In fact, the more creative and out there, the more memorable it is! It's rarely an expensive affair, which makes it all the more inclusive and fun. And, in my experience, the personal touches make for some wonderful memories for years to come.

How to plan a Swedish-style hen or stag do

Set the date Contact the other half to set a date when the person is available (without that person's knowledge, of course). The partner is then responsible for keeping that day or weekend free (it might require some double bluffing), providing a list of people who should be invited and packing a bag when the day arrives.

The brainstorm It's customary for the group to brainstorm ideas secretly. This is one of the most fun parts and a great way to get the group together. The activity suggestions usually vary from pleasant (a picnic in the park, bonding in the sauna or enjoying an activity out in nature) to crazy (writing a song and performing it on the street to collect money for your outfit for the big day).

Set and stick to a budget The budget is also a part of the wider group discussion. It's important that everyone feels comfortable with the cost and no one is excluded. After all, it's about gathering all the people who are special to the bride or groom for some pre-wedding fun. Ensure that the finances are arranged beforehand and keep within budget to make sure no one is out of pocket.

Divide up the tasks Once the activities have been determined, the responsibilities are divided up among the group. One person may take on the role of creating a playlist, another a game, and another may make the dinner reservation or prepare a picnic. The key is to ensure that no one has too much to organize. It's very much a team effort.

The kidnap The way you surprise your protagonist sets the tone. Timing and style are crucial! More often than not, the group will appear at the door or even at the end of the bed. In my experience, the bridal party usually opts for a kinder approach, but stag dos are known for the many eventful ways in which they kidnap the groom. Sometimes they even indulge in a fake kidnap, such as asking the groom to be somewhere dressed as a rabbit, only for him to wait hours before eventually returning home. The real stag do is usually a few weeks later, during which time the 'stags' have had enough laughs to last a lifetime. Cruel? Possibly. But if it's done the right way for the person you're celebrating, it can be great fun for everyone involved.

The lagom wedding

In my experience, Swedish weddings are rarely lavish. In fact, they're often beautifully simple yet truly personal. The big day is often a budget-friendly affair, smaller than the average wedding, and, as with many Swedish gatherings, the emphasis is on getting together and having fun.

This is particularly apt in this day and age when the cost of weddings is soaring in many countries – the average US wedding budget is estimated to have increased by $5,500 over the past five years,[5] reaching a total average cost of $30,000 – and that's before factoring in the honeymoon! The stress of organizing such a large event steals the focus from the marriage itself and will no doubt mean you'll begin married life in debt. In fact, a study by Emory University in Atlanta, Georgia, revealed that the more you spend on your wedding, the less time your union will last![6]

The study found that splashing out $30,000 on your big day was found to increase the odds of divorce by 250 per cent, compared to those who spend between $5,000 and $10,000. Interestingly, spending less than $1,000 gives you the best odds for a long marriage.

If this revelation isn't enough to make us want to scale back on our spending, I don't know what will be! If you're planning a wedding, here are a few ways to rein things in, give yourself the best chance of a happy wedding day and set yourself up for an even happier marriage.

A little help from your friends

People love to be involved in helping you prepare for your big day. Among your guests, there's likely to be one or more people who have a special skill or something they could contribute. Politely ask them if they'd like to be involved – but do ensure they can relax and enjoy the wedding, too!

Search your wedding-invite list and see if you know:

+ a singer
+ a photographer
+ a hairdresser

+ a makeup artist
+ someone who is good at flower arranging or some other decorative skill

Photography

I've been to many Swedish weddings where guests have helped out with the photography. Often this results in wonderfully relaxed and informal snapshots of the day – all very lagom. It's a little too much to ask your photographer friend to work at your wedding free of charge, but you might find an introverted guest with a natural interest in photography who would be more than happy to hide behind a camera now and then. Likewise, with all your guests armed and ready with compact cameras and phones, it'll be easy to create an album afterwards.

The rustic venue

Often it's the venue that costs an arm and a leg. In Sweden, people are permitted to get married anywhere they like, which gives rise to the most beautiful settings – by a lake, in a forest clearing or even up a mountain. The ceremony is followed by a wedding meal at a summer cottage, in the village hall or in the garden. The key is to keep nature at the centre. It can be a more stunning backdrop than a stately home – and it's free!

In case of rain, it's wise to have borrowed a covering of some kind to keep everyone dry. Having said that, one of the most fun weddings I've attended was one where everyone brought an umbrella and a pair of wellington boots to change into for the ceremony! If nothing else, it certainly makes for some colourful wedding photos!

Table settings

In many countries, it's customary to have a head table set apart from the rest of the party, maybe even raised to overlook the throng of guests. At a Swedish wedding, it's more common to opt for a U-shape or M-formation, where the head table is across the top and connected to the other arms. These long rows create a relaxed, social setting where guests can easily chat to those at the head table.

If you're looking to emulate a Swedish wedding, don't worry about everything looking perfect. Mismatched chairs, flowers in jam jars and twinkling candles provide a perfectly relaxed atmosphere and a pretty setting to boot.

The speeches

In Sweden, the toastmaster's role kicks in once the *bröllopsmiddag* (wedding dinner) begins. He or she organizes the speeches, of which there are many. Be it with an anecdote, a song or even a poem, guests step out of their comfort zone to pay tribute to the happy couple over the course of the evening. These thoughtful contributions add a truly personal touch.

It may be difficult to break the wedding code. For example, in the UK or US people might think it slightly odd if you give a speech when you're not the best man, father of the bride, groom, bride or part of the wedding party. But there are other ways you can add fun, unexpected elements to the proceedings. How about a Swedish wedding game?

Four Swedish wedding games

The shoe game The best man secretly asks guests to jot down a question for the bride and groom, ranging from the more mundane 'Who's in charge of the remote control?' to the more adventurous 'Who made the first move?' The pair are then asked to stand on their chairs back to back, holding a bridal shoe in one hand and a groom shoe in the other (at a same-sex wedding this works if the couple are wearing different coloured shoes). They then raise the shoe that best answers the question.

Kisses on demand! Swedes love to see the bride and groom kiss, so much so that they've invented a game to ensure it. A clink of glasses from the guests during the *bröllopsmiddag* (wedding dinner) is a cue for the couple to kiss in their seats. A united stamping of the feet is a sign they should stand on their chairs for a kiss. But if the guests bang on the table, it's time for the couple to head under the table for a kiss away from prying eyes!

You may now (all) kiss the bride At a Swedish wedding, the bride and groom might hold off on that trip to the bathroom. Traditionally, as soon as a newly-wed is out of sight, the entire room clinks their glasses and all of the opposite sex line up to give the remaining newly-wed a peck on the cheek before the other returns.

Sånghäfte **(song booklet)** I am completely tone deaf, so imagine my horror when I turned up at my first Swedish wedding to discover a booklet containing a number of ditties on my table setting! (I later found out this practice is a staple at many Swedish celebrations). The *sånghäfte* includes a series of traditional, numbered *snapsvisor* (schnapps songs). Someone in the party will call out a number, and everyone will burst into song with the help of the lyrics on the page. The end of the song is celebrated with a jovial 'Skål!' and a shot of schnapps (note: you might find your singing improves as the evening goes on).

The lagom guide
to parenting

As a mother of three, I'm the first to admit that, although rewarding, parenting is no easy feat. In a day and age when we're told we can have it all – hold down a career, be a parent and enjoy some me time – everything has become a juggling act, and we're constantly rushing about at the speed of light. We're simply doing the best we can, and it rarely feels good enough! But it doesn't have to be that way.

WE'RE NOT SUPERHUMAN

What if we realized that we don't need to be an all-singing, all-dancing super-parent to be a good parent? That our children will benefit greatly from experiencing everything in moderation, whether that's our undivided attention, time with friends, time to be bored, toys, crafts, sports, screen time, nature or learning? By placing less pressure on ourselves and our little ones, and giving them the space to blossom, we can all find greater balance.

One-on-one time

As parents, we're usually running around like crazy, attempting to balance work, home, errands and everything in between. As a result, taking time out of the day to spend it with our children – I mean really spend time with them and give them our 100-per cent undivided attention – isn't always on the agenda. But what if we start to think that spending quality time with our children doesn't have to be a jam-packed day full of activities? What if we expected less of ourselves? What if setting aside a few minutes of the day is enough to raise their self-esteem and make them feel loved, listened to and worthy?

When my children were very small, my older sister advised me that even on the busiest days I should set aside time for one activity to enjoy exclusively with them – whether it was big, like going to a museum, or small, like drawing, reading a book or doing a jigsaw puzzle together. In the spirit of lagom, providing your children with this simple but special one-on-one time is one of the best gifts you can give them. Just telling your children your door is always open if they ever need to talk or going for a walk or cycle ride together is a wonderful way to be there for them. Not only will this expectation ease the pressure on you as a parent (and that parental guilt we so often feel) but it will also give your child the attention they crave. And, more than likely, it will be the most treasured moment of the day for both of you!

Parental leave

Wander around a Swedish city on any given weekday and you'll encounter an army of men joyfully pushing prams or feeding their babies with homemade food. The so-called 'latte pappa' is a normal part of everyday life, thanks to Sweden's generous parental leave of 480 days. Parents are encouraged to share it equally, and it can be used up until the child turns 12.

My Swedish husband took six months off with our first daughter after I'd gone back to work – and I have to say the benefits were (and still are) immeasurable. I was able to return to work safe in the knowledge that my daughter was being cared for in the best possible way. And it extends to joint responsibility for doctor's appointments and after-school activities. It taught us that we're equally responsible for raising our children, and that we both have the opportunity to pursue our careers and be loving parents. It's important for our children to see this, too.

It's a common misconception in many parts of the world that women are more natural at parenting and enjoy being at home with their children more than men do. I've spoken to many men and women who have been on parental leave and discovered that enjoyment is very much dependent on the individual. I know just as many women as men who have missed going to work and even gone back earlier than planned. And I have known both men and women who found the time off a blessing and loved every minute of it. Most important, it's not about how much you enjoy it – it's about playing your part as a parent.

A survey of Americans[7] found that when people were asked about their biggest regrets in life, one of the top two was not spending enough time with family. As for children, I've learnt that they're just as happy to have mum or dad pick them up when they fall, or make them meatballs and mash and dance the morning away – so long as they've had equal access to both parents in their early years. So, let's ensure everyone is dealing with their fair share of nappy changing, scraped knees, sick days, school runs and school plays. We'll all feel happier for it!

It's good for children to be bored

'Those who wish to sing always find a song.'
Swedish proverb

It's easy to get wrapped up in the idea that our children should be constantly stimulated. But I've noticed that Swedes rarely overdo extracurricular activities. In fact, experts have confirmed that 'quiet time' is equally, if not more, important than organized activities, because it gives your child the space to develop important life skills, such as forming friendships and understanding emotions, as well as encouraging them to tap into their imaginations. So, the next time you hear your child whine, 'I'm BOOORED!' allow them to be just that. Chances are they'll come up with their most fun game yet!

THE LAGOM APPROACH TO TOYS

We all strive to make our children happy, not only providing essentials, like food, a loving home and clothes, but also ensuring they have everything they need in terms of games, toys and books. But where do we draw the line?

Our grandparents owned a small selection of toys – a bear, for example, that was highly valued and still cherished to this day. Today, our children's bedrooms are stacked with toys. But do mountains of beeping, flashing, walking and talking toys really make our little munchkins happier? I was fascinated but not surprised to learn that, according to experts, too many toys – or ones that aren't age appropriate – can actually do more harm than good.

British research showed that when children have a large number of toys they become distracted which hinders learning and play.[8] Having fewer toys gives them the chance to use their imagination and helps them treasure what they have. So the next time our little ones nag us for that plastic toy at the checkout, we can feel safe in the knowledge that we're saying no for their sake – and not because we know it will be painful to step on in the middle of the night!

So which toys should we invest in? As with all things lagom, it's about finding balance. Yes, every child needs a toy and other tools to help them play, but they also need our time, time to play with friends and time to be alone.

How to choose the right toy

When it comes to choosing toys, it's tempting to go for the bright plastic ones that (literally) call to you as you walk past. But often it's the classic toys that you get the most mileage from and that help children use their imagination the most. For example, Lego, wood blocks, train sets and other construction toys encourage little ones to think creatively and develop important motor, problem-solving, language and spatial skills.[9] Likewise, toys that stimulate imaginary play – such as wigwams, dolls' houses, train sets, play kitchens and soft plush toys – help with social learning, communication skills and cognitive and physical development.

Consider investing in beautifully made, timeless items instead of plastic so that they can be enjoyed year after year, and by the next generation, too!

Five things to look for in a toy

+ It has more than one use.
+ It stimulates exploratory play.
+ It helps the imagination.
+ It can be used as your child gets older.
+ It doesn't over entertain (i.e. flash, beep, play music).

Dressing-up box

I absolutely love seeing my children totter around in fabulous outfits they've pulled together from the dressing-up box. In my mind, the best boxes have flamboyant pieces like traditional costumes picked up on travels (the Spanish flamenco dress is a favourite in our house) and items discarded from your own wardrobe (the perfect way to dispose of that guilty purchase you've never worn), as well as vintage hats, costume jewellery and whacky sunglasses from secondhand stores. The odd feather boa is always a treat, too!

Traditional crafts

Whenever Farmor (my children's paternal grandmother) comes to visit, the girls have a field day learning traditional crafts. Ever since they were tiny, they've been finger knitting, crocheting and sewing. They've designed dolls' clothes and walk around with bags they've lovingly made with their own little hands.

These traditional crafts are not only great for developing fine motor skills but they also help the girls' concentration and imagination – plus, I see them beam with pride every time they finish something new! (Warning: you might just find yourself wearing a rainbow-coloured hat for a day or so …)

Run out of glue? Play-Doh gone dry? Not a problem! Farmor has taught us how easy it is to rustle up makeshift hobby replacements using the contents of the food cupboard. My children often make their own glue, but the most popular of all is Swedish *trolldeg*, or salt dough.

HOW TO MAKE
TROLLDEG (SALT DOUGH)

What you need

+ 200g (⅔ cup) plain flour
+ 100g (⅓ cup) salt
+ 150ml (⅔ cup) luke warm water

What to do

1. Place the flour and salt in a mixing bowl.

2. Slowly add the water and blend the mixture until it has a dough-like texture.

3. Knead the dough until it becomes pliable.

4. Shape the dough into your own creation.

5. Place the creation in the oven at 110°C/230°F/gas mark ¼ for one hour.

6. Allow it to cool at room temperature overnight.

7. Once dry, your children can bring their creation to life with hobby paint.

EVERYTHING IN MODERATION

Screen time is a hot topic in the press and among parents.
How much? When? What? But there is certainly a time and
a place for viewing. Why not make screen time fun and set
aside an evening to watch TV as a family? It's a perfect way
to cuddle up after a long week – especially if there are some
snacks involved!

Fredagsmys

I remember as a child we used to sit down at 7 p.m. every
Wednesday to watch *Dallas*. It was something I'd look forward
to each week. Not because of the show itself, of course (ahem);
I simply loved watching TV together as a family. In many
parts of the world, communal viewing is becoming less and
less common, but in Sweden it's still incredibly popular and
even has its own name: *Fredagsmys*, or Cosy Friday. *Fredagsmys*
requires a small amount of preparation (namely putting
some popcorn in the microwave) and is best enjoyed on a
large, comfy sofa. It's an evening dedicated to spending time
together and unwinding as a family after a long week – you
just need to find a show everyone can enjoy!

Recipe for a successful *Fredagsmys*

+ Set aside your phones and clear your calendar for the evening.

+ Plan a simple, popular meal that all the family loves, such as pizza or tacos.
+ Select an activity you can all do together, like playing a board game or watching a film.
+ Bring out snacks, such as popcorns and crisps, to share.

Lördagsgodis – Saturday sweets

Swedes teach their children the art of moderation from a young age. And what better way to do this than with sweets? Every Saturday, the 'sugar-overload' aisle in our local supermarket is packed with excited children picking out their *lördagsgodis* (Saturday sweets), a treat they've been looking forward to all week. Confining sugary treats to one day a week is an extremely clever concept: it's healthier (overall consumption is lowered), it teaches the art of moderation and, perhaps best of all, the anticipation makes it an extra-special occasion. Each and every bite of a lollipop, sweet and chocolate is savoured.

Sweet-truth!

Swedish children may be waiting for their weekly sugar dose, but it seems their parents don't have quite the same willpower. Recent estimates by London-based market research company Euromonitor placed Sweden in the top seven sweet-eating countries in the world per capita! (Just don't tell the kids.)

CHILDREN AND THE GREAT OUTDOORS

Let's face it: few children greet 'Let's go for a walk in the countryside' with shouts of joy. In our house, announcing an excursion of this kind is akin to telling them Father Christmas won't be coming down the chimney this year. However, once out, it's a whole different story, and I see them racing through the woods, collecting sticks and stones (usually brought home en masse), jumping over streams and rolling down hills. They'll never admit it, but they do actually enjoy it, and it's a great way to spend relaxed time together as a family without everyday distractions.

It's not always easy to set aside an entire day, but I've found it doesn't have to be a major event. Even small adventures outdoors – like running around the back garden or playing in the local park together – have equal benefits for children and the family as a whole. Many studies report the positive effects that time in nature has on our children. These include stimulating creativity and problem solving, enhancing cognitive abilities, improving nutrition (according to one study, children who spend time outdoors gardening or with a horticultural-based curriculum are more likely to eat fruit and vegetables[10]), helping them to form healthier relationships with others and improving eyesight (time outside was shown to reduce near-sightedness in children).[11] Who knew? Talk about the best things in life being free!

Ten creative activities to enjoy with children outdoors

If you're inspired to dig out the boots and join the outdoor movement but aren't sure where to start, here are a few simple activities your children will love:

Run through the alphabet, asking children to collect small pieces from the wild starting with the different letters.

Collect leaves and other lightweight items to create a collage once you're home.

Point out the names of wildflowers and birds.

Make daisy chains or dandelion crowns.

Teach children about outdoor survival (e.g. what to do if you get lost in a forest, how to light a fire from scratch) – they'll find it fascinating.

Get your hands dirty and make good old mud pies.

Build a sandcastle.

Go shell-seeking.

Sow some seeds and get your children interested in gardening – they will love to help out and get their hands dirty.

Have fun with leaf and bark rubbing.

Rowan-berry necklaces

Children love to make necklaces and bracelets, and I was fascinated to watch my Swedish neighbour Nina keep 12 young children occupied at a birthday party for a good half an hour, threading rowan berries on a string with a needle to create necklaces. Once ready, simply hang them up to dry.

Forest schools

If you're really keen for your child to get interested in the great outdoors, you might want to consider a forest school. Growing in number across the UK, this type of outdoor nursery has been available in Sweden for many years – it's designed to encourage children to learn through outdoor play all year round. Think climbing trees, eating lunch, making mud pies and even napping under the open sky, come snow, rain or shine. Sound crazy? Scientists may beg to differ.

A longitudinal study by Sarah Blackwell found long-term forest-schools programmes 'had positive impacts on children's physical and mental health in addition to improving their social and cognitive competence'[12]. Ideal! My friend Sarah-Louise, a fellow Brit living in Sweden, has chosen a forest preschool for her son. She explained: 'We love the idea of our son being outdoors in all weathers. It's meant to be great for his immune system and depleting those very high energy levels! The children even sleep in their own outdoor sleigh bed with down duvets for their morning naps.' Perhaps it's not such a crazy idea after all!

Dressing for the occasion

In Sweden, spending time outdoors with your children isn't confined to fair-weather days, and it's not usually in other countries, either. Except there's a difference: when it comes to dressing children for the weather, the Swedes have it down.

I positively marvel at the way the Swedes dress their children for the weather. Every season brings with it a new collection of appropriate attire, be it a full-body snowsuit, rain overalls and boots or a spring hat.

I experienced this first hand one morning at my daughter's nursery. 'She has no "outer trousers",' the teacher said as she wagged her finger at me one October. I explained that she did indeed have both a pair of rain trousers and snow trousers. 'No, no,' the teacher said, somewhat exasperated. 'She needs trousers that are somewhere in between.' Frustrated, I consulted a friend who confirmed that she was referring to a type of hardwearing 'play trouser' pulled on over skirts, dresses or trousers before playtime to protect clothes. Mothers and fathers everywhere, rejoice! Imagine this simple, practical way to prevent clothes getting wet, grass-stained or ripped during playground antics? Not to mention the children getting to go wild and truly let their hair down – no matter what the weather.

The lagom guide to dressing your child for the weather

+20°C (68°F)

+ Sun hat and neck cover
+ Sunscreen
+ Sunglasses
+ Rash vest (if on beach)
+ Feet covers such as surf shoes
  or wetsuit shoes (if on the beach)
+ Cool top with long sleeves
  (or covering the shoulders)

5–15°C (40–60°F) everyday

+ Tough, waterproof trousers
+ Thin gloves
+ Thin hat

5–15°C (40–60°F) and rain

+ Waterproof trousers
+ Waterproof anorak
  with hood
+ Wellington boots

-0° (32°F) and snow

+ Base layer
+ Mid layer
+ Outer layer
+ Ski socks
+ Snowsuit
+ Scarf or neckwarmer
+ Waterproof snow boots

LEARNING THE LAGOM WAY

It's amazing how many parents teach their children to read and write before school starts. When I visit the UK, I inevitably hear, 'Lila's seven but has a reading age of thirteen.' Yawn! I might be missing the point – of course it's great that they are so advanced – but what seven-year-old wants to read a book written for a thirteen-year-old?

One of the many things I love about Swedish parenting is this: I very rarely experience any competitiveness or parents boasting about their children learning to read or write before school age. Furthermore, I once asked my child's Swedish preschool teacher if there was anything I could do to help my children develop at home. 'You be the parent, we'll be the teacher,' she advised. Not only has this made me feel much calmer (trust me, I do get into a panic when I get back from the UK – 'We've got to do some writing!') but it also means I'm less likely to put pressure on my children. If they initiate reading and writing, sure – we give them a helping hand. But let's teach them the important things first, like saying thank you and being a good friend. The rest can follow at school.

Three important things to teach your children before school

+ How to be a good friend
+ How to share
+ How to be thankful

'Don't educate your
children to be rich.
Educate them to be happy,
so they know the value of
things, not the price.'

Victor Hugo

Letting your child take the lead

'Even the smallest of stars shines in the darkness.'
Swedish proverb

⌇⌇⌇

Swedish children start compulsory school the year they turn
seven, two years later than their UK counterparts. Up until
then, the focus is purely on play. This may sound late (and
I was certainly concerned), but studies actually show that
children who start learning to read and write later are no less
successful than peers who start earlier.[13] Plus, the later readers
and writers showed signs of greater well-being.

To me, this makes total sense. As a parent, I've noticed
that when my girls are naturally ready to do something – be it
walk, potty train, ride a bike or decipher letters – they master it
quickly. Try to teach them before they're ready, and it causes a
huge amount of stress and aggravation. The process becomes
long and drawn out, and may even prove futile. So let's slow
down and take things at our children's pace. We'll all feel
happier for it!

Ease the pressure

This slower way of learning continues throughout primary
school. The focus is on learning without the pressure to
succeed by achieving top grades. 'It's about helping children
discover the pleasure of learning, often working together in

pairs or groups, rather than insisting they compete against one another,' enthuses my British friend Joanna Le Pluart, who studied history at Cambridge and whose daughters have grown up in the Swedish school system.

Of course, we can't control the age at which our children start compulsory school nor the teaching philosophy, but we can think about the pressures we place on our children. A lagom approach is to guide and encourage our children, but first to show them unconditional love, be non-judgmental and accept they'll have strengths and weaknesses. And then we watch them fly as well-rounded adults.

A sentence to say to your child

As a parent, it's natural to want to praise your children for their efforts and performance. Instead, Bruce Brown – coach, presenter and author behind *The Role of Parents in Athletics* – suggests using six simple words to help children perform well and amplify their positive memories of the game: 'I love to watch you play.' He says: 'It is part of our concept of being able to "release your kids to healthy activities" – all the success and challenges belong to them and we are there to watch and encourage but not interfere.' Sound words, indeed!

Pink and blue

Hen (hEn): a gender-neutral personal
pronoun intended as an alternative to the
gender-specific *hon* (she) and *han* (he).[14]

I have fallen foul of many a gender faux pas. 'Isn't your little
girl sweet,' I would say to the Swedish mother of a baby
dressed head to toe in pink. 'It's a he' would be the perplexed
response. It might just be me, but I often find that without
the gender 'appropriate' clothing, it's almost impossible to tell
whether a baby is a boy or a girl. But, as I learnt, that's entirely
the point. Take away the gender identifier, and people treat
you without any preconceived notions.

Known for being the most gender-equal country in the
world, Sweden believes that gender equality starts from the day
you're born. The idea is that the baby should be introduced
to the world without gender-specific toys or clothing. Instead,
you encourage them to enjoy the world around them based on
their natural preferences. In my eyes, there's a lot to be said
for providing your children with opportunities, regardless of
sex. Yes, at the end of the day, some girls may still gravitate
towards dolls and some boys towards trucks – but there'll be
many more who won't, and that's perfectly OK, too. So let's
stop thinking 'pink' and 'blue', and categorizing toys into
those for 'boys' or 'girls'. Let's start allowing children to be
children, whatever their preference.

The lagom guide
to celebrations

Never is the lagom philosophy more evident than with celebrations. Christmas, Easter and midsummer tend to be relaxed affairs, geared towards being together, keeping the costs down and sharing the load. Gifts are carefully selected to be just right for the occasion and wrapped in simple, understated paper. Decoration is an equally delicate balance – overdo it, and it will be considered vulgar, underdo it, and it won't look *festligt* (party-like).

CHRISTMAS

Every year our family celebrates Christmas twice – once with the Swedish side of the family and once in London. So not lagom, I know, but since neither my husband nor I was ready to skip our annual family Christmas, we agreed this was the best solution! Each festive occasion is wonderful in its own way. In Sweden, it's celebrated on December 24 and centred around a fantastic *julbord* (Christmas table) – a buffet bursting with Swedish delicacies like pickled herrings, eggs, Jansson's temptation (potato with anchovies), meatballs, and many, many other foods.

Although we all have our traditions – and perhaps I'm not quite ready to swap a turkey for pickled herring – I admire the way my family-in-law organizes the event. Each person is responsible for bringing something to the table, quite literally.

I've noticed that helping out and contributing food and drink to a big event is common at all Swedish celebrations – whether it's the aforementioned *julbord* or a midsummer table. Dividing up tasks not only takes the pressure off the host but also means everyone has a sense of responsibility for making the day great. In essence, by sharing out responsibility for dishes, drinks, children's food, music, a quiz and even a treasure hunt, everyone has a lagom amount to do, no one is out of pocket, and everyone enjoys a more relaxed affair.

Understated decorations

When it comes to Christmas decorations in Sweden, there's a distinct serenity and cosiness, and also a strong sense of nostalgia. On the whole, coloured flashing lights and Father Christmas climbing up the side of the house are strictly out of bounds. I don't even want to imagine what would happen if you placed a 10-foot inflatable snowman in your garden. No. When it comes to decorating lagom style, think flickering candles, delicate fairy lights with a soft, off-white glow, vintage decorations and tablecloths that have been passed down from generation to generation, as well as handmade and natural touches from outside your door.

The rustic Christmas tree

In the days running up to Christmas, there's usually a tree frenzy, with everyone in search of the perfect pine – not too tall, too short, too stout, too asymmetrical, too bushy or too sparse. But what if I said: the more imperfect the tree, the better?

Since many Swedes chop down their own trees, it can be a case of using whatever's grown in the garden over the year. But even if the tree is selected from a farm or a local store, there's still an emphasis on imperfection. In fact, some even shun the conical-shaped pine for a Lebanese cedar tree (also very popular in Denmark). It's fairly spartan, often crooked and far from perfect, but it's incredibly charming and has many benefits. The spacing between the branches means you can see each decoration more clearly, and it also allows space for real candles.

By picking up an imperfect tree you'll add a bucket-load of rustic charm to your home at Christmas. But for an extra Swedish touch, search online for 'Scandinavian Christmas tree' inspiration – you'll find the internet awash with images of trees in wicker baskets. It took me some time to learn how to recreate this look. The trick is to find a tree planted in a pot rather than chopped off at the stem. If you manage to get a tree with roots, even better – you can replant it in your garden for next Christmas!

Chopping down your Christmas tree

With so much forest on their doorstep, it's not uncommon for Swedes to chop down a tree in their garden or visit a nearby Christmas-tree farm. Since moving to Sweden, I've preferred heading out to a tree farm with a saw over selecting one in the supermarket car park. Our annual tree-chopping ceremony is accompanied by a load of warm clothes (see pages 82 and 86), a Thermos of *glögg* (a form of mulled wine) and *pepparkakor* (ginger thins – see page 192). Needless to say, it's one of our favourite days of the whole year!

Sustainable Christmas-tree farms are becoming increasingly popular across Europe and beyond, so why not look for one in your area and make chopping down your tree a new tradition? Nothing beats the smell of fresh pine and the sense of achievement – plus, by choosing the right farm, you'll know it's from a sustainable source.

Think outside the sitting room!

It's easy to think a Christmas tree should be confined to the corner of the sitting room. But since moving to Sweden, I've been inspired by the practice of placing mini trees in other parts of the house, too. Whether in the bedroom (oh so cosy to wake up to!), on the coffee table, in the window or even on the stairs, there's no end to where you might place one. My children love having their own mini trees in their bedrooms, and they make handmade decorations for them (with varying results!). You can also place them either side of your front door for a warm welcome. Forget fancy decorations – leave them *au naturel* or add a simple string of white fairy lights to brighten up the darkest of corners.

Real Christmas-tree candles

Real candles were the only option before electrical fairy lights took over. And, lately, people have been taking a leaf from times gone by and reverting to the real deal. We had wax candles on our tree for the first time last Christmas, and, I have to say, it looked truly magical. Since they're only lit for half an hour or so at a time, it becomes a bit of an occasion as the family gathers around to enjoy them. Also, since you can't leave the tree unattended, you need to stand or sit and watch it for the best part of 30 minutes before blowing out the candles again – which is surprisingly mindful. And, most important of all, the soft glow of candlelight nestled between the pine needles is a truly beautiful sight. I wholeheartedly recommend it! Don't forget to stay safe – be vigilant, always keep a bucket of sand by the tree, ensure candles are placed well away from the branches above and never leave the tree unattended when candles are lit.

Vintage decorations

In Sweden, it's not uncommon to decorate the tree with flag garlands and little treasures made from wood, tin and glass that have been passed down from generation to generation. Why not have a rummage around your local flea markets in the run-up to the holiday season and give forgotten items a new lease of life? The more mismatched, the better!

Crafting

Swedes love to *pysslar* (get creative) before any big holiday. They generally set aside a day to make decorations and bake as a family. To *julpysslar* (create Christmas crafts) may involve making a gingerbread house (see page 193), a candle wreath (see page 190) or paper stars to hang on the tree. The beauty is that the creation doesn't have to be perfect – in fact, the more rustic, the better. It's simply about getting together and enjoying the moment.

Natural handmade decorations

Many Swedes like to forage for seasonal items like pine cones, holly sprigs, boxwood and acorn cups, which they'll then use to create centrepieces, a wreath and little decorative touches for all over the home. Traditionally, Christmas decorations start to go up on the first day of Advent, although subtle, homemade seasonal wreaths on the door offer a warm welcome long before this. Natural homemade decorations are very much about keeping the look simple and letting the shape of the leaves and the scent of the freshly cut foliage speak for itself.

TWO SIMPLE CHRISTMAS DECORATIONS
INSPIRED BY NATURE

To create an immediate sense of holiday spirit, hang a homemade wreath on your door or in the window. It doesn't have to be complicated – in fact, the simpler it is, the more charming and inviting it will feel!

The hanging-candle wreath

A single flickering candle in the window can brighten up even the darkest of days. This simple candle wreath is relatively easy to create and looks beautiful hanging in the window. Once finished, light the candle and watch it twinkle in the dark.

What you need

+ A bundle of eucalyptus foliage (you can also use boxwood, spruce or anything else that is in season and readily available)
+ Green garden wire
+ Wire cutters
+ Round metal frame (a coat hanger bent into shape will also do!) approximately 35cm (14in) diameter or larger, depending on the candle you would like to use
+ Leather or twine for hanging
+ Clip-on candle holder
+ Small candle

What to do

1. Take three sprigs of foliage and bind them together at the stem using the garden wire.

2. Use wire to fix the stems of the bundle to the metal frame.

3. Create a new foliage bundle and overlap the tips with the first bundle to hide the wire, then fasten them in place with more wire.

4. Continue until you've covered half of the circle.

5. Measure the height at which you would like to hang the wreath and then attach the appropriate length of leather string or twine to the centre of the top half of the metal frame – the uncovered half – using a small knot. Cut away the excess.

6. Add the clip-on candleholder to the centre of the bottom half of the wreath – the half that is covered in foliage – and fix the candle in the holder. Hang the wreath vertically in your window and watch it twinkle!

Ice tea-light holders

These ice tea-light holders are a lovely way to light up a path or add a twinkle to your doorstep. To make your own, pour water into a bowl or plant pot until it's half full. Then add a handful of greenery to the water. Take a second bowl and place it inside the first bowl of water (being careful not to press it all the way down). If temperatures are below zero, leave them outside or, if not, place them in the freezer. Wait for the water to freeze (the length of time depends on the amount of water you've used and the conditions, but to err on the safe side leave overnight) before carefully removing both bowls. Add a tea light and enjoy seeing them brighten up the darkness.

Pepparkakor, or ginger thins

'One becomes kind from ginger thins.'
Swedish proverb

No Christmas in Sweden would be complete without *pepparkakor.* Dating back to the 14th century, *pepparkakor* are crunchy ginger thins with notes of cinnamon, ginger and cloves. Traditionally, they were thought to have medicinal properties, and according to Swedish folklore, your wish will come true if you hold a ginger thin in the palm of your hand, gently tap its centre and it breaks into three pieces.They are sometimes handmade but more often bought, and you can enjoy them plain or (my favourite) with cheese and a dollop of fig jam, washed down with a steaming mug of hot cocoa or *glögg,* a form of Swedish mulled wine.

Children are sometimes invited to carve out different-shaped *pepparkakor,* using cookie cutters, before decorating them with white icing or simply leaving them natural. And if you're feeling creative, you can buy them with a hole in place and create the sweetest of sweet decorations to hang on the Christmas tree or in a cluster in the kitchen. Alternatively, you can decorate a name on the ginger thin to create edible gift tags – it's a deliciously sweet addition to your gift wrapping.

Gingerbread house

Why not take your *pepparkakor* craft skills to the next level and make a gingerbread house? Whether it's a miniature house to enjoy with a hot chocolate and marshmallows or an entire estate, the only limit is your imagination. And if all else fails, you can eat it before anyone sees it. What have you got to lose?

EASTER

As with most holidays, the Swedish house before *påsk* (Easter) is a hive of activity. Easter decorations come out of the attic, feathers are tied to bushes outside the door, and little eggs hang from branches in the garden and in a prime spot inside. Often, the family will also set aside a day for *påskpysslar* (Easter crafting) to add a handmade touch before the children dress up as *påskkärringar* (little Easter witches) and go around the neighbourhood with a basket collecting sweets. Do the latter in your country and they might think you've lost your mind! But there are some Swedish traditions that are easy to recreate.

Egg dying

Who doesn't love dying eggs at Easter time? Most of the time you don't need to follow a tutorial – simply hard-boil your eggs and dip them into a food-colouring dye and arrange them in a bowl for an instant seasonal touch! Or, if you want to go that eggs-tra (sorry!) mile, replace the food colouring with dye made from non-toxic natural products. Experiment with the different foods and look online for recipes to create the colours you need.

Egg rolling

My children enjoy this game every year on Easter day at their Swedish grandparents' house (I have to say, it's fun as an adult, too – my husband and I get quite competitive!). There are many versions of the game, but we tend to hard-boil a dozen eggs, climb to the top of a hill and roll the eggs down it. The person whose egg gets the furthest wins. (You can repeat until your egg completely falls apart or choose to eat it before it gets to that fateful stage.)

Äggpickning – egg scrambling

Also known as egg scrambling, *äggpickning* is a traditional Easter game played by two or more players. First, the participants hard-boil and paint or dye their eggs. Then the aim is to knock or 'peck' the top of the other's unshelled egg until one of them cracks. If there are more than two people involved, the winners go through to the next round.

Easter table decorations

It's incredible the lengths to which some Swedes will go to get that Easter vibe at home: I've even seen curtains decorated with chicks and eggs! On the whole, however, effortless yet fun touches are key, and they are relatively easy to achieve.

MIDSUMMER

I first visited Sweden when I was nine years old, and one of my earliest memories is wearing a wildflower crown in my hair and dancing around a maypole. Unbeknownst to me, I was participating in one of the biggest events in the Swedish calendar: midsummer. Since the Swedes are a very practical nation, the summer solstice is celebrated on the Friday between 19 and 25 June. Traditionally, midsummer was connected to magic, and gathering wildflowers was seen as a way to secure nature's magical powers to ensure good health for the rest of the year.

Today, villagers gather together to erect a large maypole decorated with wild flowers. Girls with floral crowns, boys and adults alike then dance around the maypole to tunes such as *Små Grodorna* ('The Little Frogs') to celebrate the warm weather (not always the case) and long days. After the revelry, everyone tucks into a feast of herring, potatoes, strawberries and other delicacies. It's fast become one of my favourite events of the year, thanks to the simple, rustic nature of the day. There are no gifts and no frivolities – it's just a time to get together with all generations and revel in the abundance of daylight.

A guide to celebrating midsummer

You don't need a midsummer pole to celebrate the longest day of the year. Why not gather family and friends on the summer solstice, put flowers in your hair and enjoy supper al fresco to drink in the light and celebrate warmth and sunshine?

However, if you would like to go all out and celebrate the Swedish way, here are a few key ingredients you need to think about:

+ **Invite friends** and family over for the summer solstice.

+ **Make your own** midsummer pole (there are plenty of YouTube clips on how to do this!) and decorate with leaves entwined with wild flowers.

+ **Create** floral crowns together for the girls in the group (see page 198).

+ **Play** some music and dance around the pole (occasionally hopping like a frog!).

+ **Enjoy** an al fresco feast of herring, potatoes and strawberries washed down with beer and schnapps. (You may want to plan for an awning and blankets in case of bad weather – as is tradition at midsummer!)

+ **Create** song sheets of a series of fun, short ditties and encourage the group to sing intermittently during the course of the meal.

HOW TO MAKE
A FLORAL CROWN

What you need

+ Garden wire
+ Wire cutters
+ Tape measure

+ Green foliage
+ An assortment of freshly picked wild blooms with stems cut to 8cm (3in) lengths

What to do

1. Take a length of wire and form it into a circle, leaving the ends loose.

2. Measure the crown of your head to see how big the circular shape needs to be and use the wire cutters to remove excess wire.

3. Tie the ends of the circle together ensuring there are no sharp edges.

4. Wrap green foliage around the circle and secure into place using wire.

5. Add a bloom and secure into place with the garden wire.

6. Overlap the stem of a bloom with a new flower until you come full circle.

Midsummer romance

Swedish tradition dictates that if a single woman gathers seven different types of flowers and places them under her pillow on midsummer day, she'll dream of the man she's going to marry.

HOW TO BE A LAGOM GUEST!

Invited to a celebration? Why not channel the Swedes and pride yourself on being the perfect guest? Simple steps like offering to contribute something to the event, turning up on time and bearing a thoughtful present will have your host positively beaming and set the tone for a wonderful time.

The lagom gift

My husband always puts the brakes on my dinner-party gifts and gets slightly panicked at the sight of more than one. Having experienced Swedish gift exchanges over the years, I now understand that it's extremely important not to go over the top, which will inevitably embarrass the recipient and show up the other guests. It's also important not to bring too little (or to go empty-handed). In other words, the present should be just right for the occasion. Quite often, guests will arrive armed with thoughtful, handmade gifts, which I've found are the most valued of all. It means that someone has put time, effort and thought into creating it just for you, and it's nearly always unique!

Three homemade gifts your friends will love

+ **A bouquet of seasonal herbs:** pick a selection of herbs from your garden and bind them with plain brown string and place in a jam jar with water. Write a little note saying which herbs they are

and that once the roots come through, they can plant them in
their garden. Who doesn't love the scent of thyme, rosemary
and mint on a summer's day?

+ **Cake in a jar:** treat your friend to something delicious! Layer
the ingredients for a batch of brownies or another favourite bake
in a jar and note the recipe on a gift tag so they can make it
themselves on a rainy day.

+ **Sow a seed** in a simple terracotta pot and provide care
instructions. Your friend can watch the seedling grow and,
if it's edible, enjoy it for lunch at harvest time.

Au naturel gift wrapping

Invite friends over for a celebration, and they'll arrive with beautifully wrapped gifts. What sets Swedish present wrapping apart is that they'll forgo ostentatious ribbons and expensive wrapping paper in favour of understated natural brown or white paper (or even newspaper) tied with simple brown garden string or traditional black-and-white twine. But mundane it's not! A delicate bloom from the garden adds a touch of colour and a divine scent on someone's birthday. Or, at Christmas, cinnamon sticks or mini pine cones offer the perfect replacement for an expensive bow.

Design your own gift wrap

Take gift wrapping one step further and decorate the paper with white or gold stickers. Or have some fun with a traditional potato stamp to create your very own design!

The lagom cards/gift label

You'll never see Swedes spend hours in a card shop. They simply don't 'do' cards like we do in the UK. Swedish cards tend to be of the one-sided postcard variety or a simple parcel label. Being British, this is a style I find hard to adopt. Having said that, with my children attending birthday parties almost weekly and plenty of our own friends celebrating being another year older, I have saved an immense amount of time and money not using the card shop.

If you're running late for a friend's birthday and don't have time to buy a card, you can always follow the Swedish approach and attach a simple postage label (white or neutral will do) to the present. Add a drawing or stickers, or use a stamp to personalize it, and take the time to write a thoughtful message.

Staying overnight?

In Sweden, it's customary to offer to bring your own bedding when visiting a friend or relative, especially at their summer cottage where there might not be enough linen to go round (or a washing machine for after you've left). If you're staying overnight, why not offer to bring your own linen? It won't create any more effort on your side, but it eases the burden on the host, who doesn't need to spend your arrival day making up beds and your departure day in a space akin to a Chinese laundry room. Less work all round!

03

Lagom in the wider world

The lagom guide
to community spirit

There's a conscious unselfishness about lagom, and it goes back to Viking times. Back then, it meant taking small sips of mead to ensure there was enough to go around. Today, it can be linked to working towards a fairer society as a whole, ensuring no one goes without. Whether you volunteer, donate money or generally make an effort to be kind to those around you, by working collectively we can foster a healthier, happier community.

THINKING OF OTHERS

It's easy to wander around in our own little bubble, especially
when we're drowning in a sea of emails, after-school activities,
gym classes and social events. In fact, we're often so caught
up in our own troubles that we forget to consider how others
might be dealing with their own struggles. According to a
Swedish proverb, 'One must learn to make others happy if one
wants to be happy.' And there's wisdom in this – a Harvard
Business School study[1] showed that helping other people does
indeed make you happier (perhaps because all your niggling
concerns stop feeling quite so all-important!).

Helping those in need

In general, I find Swedes to be a little shy, especially in public. You rarely receive a smile from a stranger (especially in the bigger cities), and few words are exchanged on the street. But behind this rather cool veneer is a heart of gold.

Take, for example, Sweden's reputation as Europe's most welcoming country for refugees. According to Migrationsverket, the Swedish Migration Agency, almost 163,000 people sought asylum in Sweden in 2015. A study assessing views towards 'refugees, diversity and nationalist sentiment' by Pew Research Center based in Washington, DC found Sweden to be the most positive of all European countries, with 62 per cent believing that refugees help make the nation stronger by contributing work and talent.[2]

This open-mindedness is reinforced with compassion and a willingness to help, with Swedes stepping forward in droves to offer support to new arrivals. I observed first hand all the volunteers waiting at Malmö train station to give refugees a warm welcome. Many more donated clothes, food and time to organizations, helping them settle in the country.

With so many in need of shelter and support, we can all learn something from this and take action in our own communities. Look out for volunteer groups and see if a few hours of your time can help someone in need.

'A monthly meet-up with a family who recently fled to Sweden has given my family and me a better understanding of others and also helped us to be more open-minded. We realized that we are the same. We all want what is best for our children. And sometimes people need to sacrifice a lot in order to achieve that.'

Malin Nihlberg, volunteer at Kompis Sverige, a Swedish non-profit organization working with integration

Become a volunteer

We're all aware that volunteer work is a wonderful way to give something back to our community, but it's often a nagging thought at the back of the mind – just another item on the long list of things we'd like to do. A common misconception is that we need lots of spare time to participate in activities. In fact, there's a wide variety of volunteer work out there. It doesn't have to take up a lot of your time, plus you'll gain a sense of pride and help a cause immeasurably. Time to sow that seed!

Five great ways to help
in your community

Visit a care home and ask if there's anything you can do to help. Offering one hour a week to talk with seniors can really lift their spirits, and you'll no doubt learn a lot, too.

Help out at a children's sports club – be it mucking in on the pitch or simply helping to serve hot dogs at half time to raise money.

Visit the local library and sign up to a support group. You could end up helping people new to the country learn the language.

Find a local charity you're particularly interested in. Ask how you can help.

Contact your local authority and ask about volunteer opportunities in your area. See if something piques your interest.

RANDOM ACTS OF KINDNESS

As with all things lagom, spreading a little happiness doesn't need to involve grand gestures. Sometimes the most ordinary acts add the most meaning and inspire the greatest smiles of all.

When my second daughter was born, a Swedish friend turned up at the door with a family meal and insisted she wasn't staying, so as not to disturb. Another particularly busy friend of mine dropped in to make me a cup of tea when I injured my leg – every day of the week! These simple, thoughtful acts lifted my spirits on the hardest of days.

I'm sure you're already a very caring person, but sometimes a gentle reminder to be aware of others doesn't go amiss. And often catching people off-guard with an unexpected act of kindness can be the most touching gesture of all.

Freecycle!

Last year, my daughter left her tricycle outside the front door with a note saying, 'I've outgrown my tricycle. Please take it if you need it.' Later that day, the tricycle had gone and in its place was a bunch of bananas with a note (in Swedish): 'Thank you so much, Alice. You've made a little girl very happy – we hope you like bananas!' The thought of this simple exchange still makes me smile today.

Five random acts
of kindness

Why not light up someone's day? Here are a few simple ideas:

Leave a kind note in a library book for the next reader.

Decide to give out ten heartfelt compliments in a day.

Write a thank-you note to the public services, like the police, firemen or nurses.

Write a handwritten letter to a friend or relative you haven't been in touch with for years.

Carry a spare umbrella and hand it over to a friend when it rains.

'Do small things with great love. It's not how much we do, but how much love we put in the doing.'

Mother Teresa

The lagom guide to respecting nature

The Earth's surface is being disrupted at a rapid rate. Urbanization, excavation, deforestation and landfill are just some of the ways our actions threaten our health and the survival of wildlife. It's sad to think that our activities are having a harmful effect on the planet and on other living species, even leading to extinction in some cases.

ATTRACTING THE BIRDS AND THE BEES

No, not that kind of 'birds and the bees' (we've already covered that on page 144). I'm talking about all the creatures, great and small, with whom we share the planet. Put simply, we need them, and with so many species now under threat, it's vitally important that we try to give them a helping hand. It's wonderful if you have access to acres of untouched land on your doorstep, but there are also things you can do to help wildlife in your neighbourhood, even in the smallest of outdoor spaces. By helping to preserve the ecosystem, you're doing your bit to create a haven for insects, hedgehogs, birds and wildflowers.

'The wildlife and its habitat cannot speak, so we must and we will.'

Theodore Roosevelt

Go wild

At our family summer cottage, my mother-in-law leaves sections of the lawn completely untouched. Used to perfectly manicured lawns, I was somewhat bemused by the 'overgrown' look and offered to cut the grass on more than one occasion (which was politely declined). Then I learnt that there's a very sound principle behind this. Untouched areas provide a place for wildlife to go about their work undisturbed. Long grass, for example, is akin to a mini-jungle, helping to nurture flowers, pollen and seeds, and in turn attracting insects, moths, grasshoppers and larger animals like hedgehogs and birds. Likewise, a discarded pile of logs makes an ideal haven for small critters, and larger animals such as bats, birds and badgers will closely follow.

Your neighbours might think you've lost the plot if you allow the entire garden to look like an overgrown jungle, but how about devoting small sections of it to wildlife, as nature intended? After all, meadow flowers look beautiful on a summer's day, and who doesn't love a passing hedgehog?

Go native and diverse

You'll attract more wildlife when you have a diverse range of trees, shrubs and plants in your garden. Stick to native plant species to ensure nothing becomes too dominant and everything thrives.

Add a water feature

A pond, birdbath or even a container of water can help attract aquatic creatures like frogs and toads, as well as passing birds and other wildlife, to your outdoor space.

Feed the birds

Give birds a helping hand by leaving out a little food. Opt for a variety of feeders (like plates and nets, or the seed cakes on page 218) to attract more species, and keep the supply well stocked. You might even take up bird watching as a result – and join the scores of Swedish hipsters who wander the woods with a pair of binoculars!

HOW TO MAKE
A DIY WINTER BIRD FEEDER

Seed cakes are popular with birds in the winter when naturally found bird food is scarce. Create your own using a few basic ingredients and hang them from branches when the temperatures start to drop below freezing. You'll have a wonderful variety of birds flocking to your garden before you know it!

What you need

+ 200g (⅔ cup) lard
+ 400g (1⅓ cups) (approx.) bird seed
+ a knitting needle or other pointed object
+ a piece of string

What to do

1. Slightly soften the lard by leaving it in a warm place for an hour or so (do not allow it to melt, though).

2. Once softened, cut the lard into small pieces (about the size of walnuts) and place in a bowl or on a clean board. Gradually work in small handfuls of bird seed until it looks compact and the seeds stick together. Though it is quite a messy procedure, it is more easily done by hand.

3. Mould all the lard and seeds together, then shape into roundish cakes (you should be able to make six, approximately) about the size of slightly flattened tennis balls.

4. Leave in the fridge to harden overnight.

5. Remove from the fridge and make a hole in the cake using a knitting needle or other pointed instrument.

6. Thread a piece of string through the hole and hang the seed cake outside from a branch or hook – and watch the birds enjoy their feast!

Birds can become dependent on food supplies, so make sure you stock up regularly!

The insect hotel

With urban areas expanding to accommodate the growing
population, many insects are losing their homes. The Swedish
city of Mölndal has taken great measures to combat the
creepy-crawly housing shortage: a vast insect hotel designed
to attract and accommodate butterflies, birds, wild bees and
a host of other critters.

As much as you love animals, if you live in a home with
a small garden, you'll most likely want to reserve most of
your space for a glass of prosecco in the sun! But why not
also consider your own small insect hotel? They come in
all different shapes and sizes, and are a perfect way to invite
creepy-crawlies to join in the fun. They also provide some
evening entertainment – you never know who might have
moved in!

Help save the bees!

There's been a rapid decline in the number of bees since
the 1990s due to industrial agriculture, parasites and climate
change. We should all be concerned about our black-and-yellow
friends. According to the Swedish Beekeeping Association,
76 per cent of everything grown in Europe can be attributed to
pollination and the hard work of bees. Imagine a world without
apples, plums, cherries, peaches and nectarines!

With the advent of pesticide use in the countryside, urban areas have become a bee's friend. In Stockholm, there are hopes that a 'bee-friendly zone' – including a good supply of forage and water from spring to autumn – will help stop the decline. In other cities, such as Malmö, beehives are popping up on the rooftops!

Simple ways to help save the bees

All over the world beekeepers are working to support the dwindling bee population and they need our support. Here are four things you can do today:

+ Buy local honey and support the beekeepers in your area.
+ Stick to honey labelled 'non-heated' or 'non-transformed'.
+ Select organic honey.
+ You can also create a bee-friendly garden by planting some of the species on pages 222–223:

Bee-loving flowers
and plants

+ Fruits and vegetables
blackberries, cucumbers, pumpkins,
strawberries, wild garlic

+ Annuals
borage, cleome, clover, marigold,
poppy, sunflower

+ Perennials
buttercup, crocus, dahlia, foxglove,
geranium, rose, snowdrop

+ Herbs
catnip, coriander, fennel, lavender,
mint, sage, thyme

'When one tugs
at a single thing in
nature, he finds it
attached to the rest
of the world.'

John Muir

Protect the trees

It's not uncommon to own areas of wooded land in Sweden – after all, forests cover more than 50 per cent of the country (although, of course, according to the law of *allemansrätten* everyone has right of access to amble and forage). Owning a section of land with many trees comes with a large amount of responsibility, and Swedes take this responsibility seriously.

'We receive advice on how to protect, manage and nurture the forest to ensure the ecosystem thrives,' says family friend Yvonne Larsson, who owns 16 acres of forested land. 'We are conscious that how we look after our land plays a role in climate change.' As with many environmental issues, there is a continuous tussle between industry and the environment, and the Swedish Society for Nature Conservation (SSNC) is working hard to protect the forests.

If you're lucky enough to own land with trees, think before you go for the chop. You see, trees are our friends. They supply oxygen, clean the air, protect wildlife and help prevent soil erosion. In warm countries, they can also help to keep your home cool by providing shade. Natural air con? Now that's not bad!

Keep your community tidy

As we've seen earlier (see pages 16–18), Swedes are incredibly tidy people. Their fervour for orderliness extends to the public domain, too. Put simply, Sweden is pretty immaculate. There are government clean-up services, but this doesn't diminish the effort people put in to doing their bit. The Swedes take pride in helping to keep public spaces clean, whether it's leaving meeting rooms exactly as they find them or picnic spaces without a trace of rubbish. 'In Sweden, we're very proud of nature and feel a strong connection to it,' explains my friend Ulrika Sjöström. 'Leaving somewhere the way you would expect to find it is a mark of respect to others, as it allows them to enjoy the environment in the same way you did.'

It's well known that rubbish can be incredibly harmful to wildlife and the ecosystem. Rather alarmingly, Swedish environmental educator Ann Nerlund tells me, 'By 2050 it's predicted that all sea birds and many fish will contain plastic from rubbish that ends up in the oceans.' This is part of a wider issue, of course – but by tidying up after ourselves, we can do our bit to ensure that no animals suffer from our visit.

If you'd like to be proactive, look out for forthcoming community events, like park clean-ups, and take family and friends along to pick up litter.

Reduce your packaging waste

Eco-minded Sweden had already introduced payment for grocery-store plastic bags when I arrived way back in 2004. In the intervening years, many countries have followed suit, including the UK in 2015, and it's now common to see people around the world using reusable shopping bags (which is a great start). Packaging, on the other hand, continues to be a huge problem. In 2015, food packaging and containers accounted for 45 per cent of items going to US landfill.[3] With many supermarket products double or triple wrapped, and given that takeaway lattes in disposable cups are such a popular habit, it's easy to go through a vast amount of packaging.

Simple ways to minimize your packaging waste today

+ Opt for items that are returnable or refillable.
+ Go for bulk buys rather than individually wrapped items.
+ Use your own water bottle instead of plastic ones.
+ Take a travel mug with you to coffee shops to avoid disposable cups.
+ Make your favourite brew from loose-leaf tea rather than teabags.

Recycling

Recycling is nothing new, but it's certainly important to remind ourselves just how important it is. By sorting and recycling our rubbish, we're ensuring that as many materials as possible are being reused, reducing the need to extract raw materials and limiting the amount of waste that ends up in landfill and our oceans. In Sweden, there's a well-implemented recycling system in place, and an incredible 99 per cent of household waste is recycled.

Reuse your rubbish

You might even like to tap into your inner creative and give your rubbish a new lease of life – or ask a local school if they need any craft supplies. I've noticed that at my children's school there's no end to what they can make from cardboard tubes, milk cartons and aluminium foil (although it can be a job fitting everything they've made on your bike at the end of term!).

The lagom guide to saving energy at home

You only have to turn on the news to see the rapid, human-induced changes happening in our climate. It's easy to think that small gestures like recycling, conscious buying and reducing waste are futile when there are power stations spewing out toxins left, right and centre. But what if, like our heavily engaged Swedish friends, we felt our actions could make a difference? What if each and every one of us took small steps to lead a more lagom life, taking only what we need and thereby reducing the level of toxins released into the environment bit by bit? Imagine what we could achieve together!

START SMALL

'A journey of a thousand miles
always begins with a single step.'
Swedish proverb

These days I call Western Harbour – a small pocket of
Malmö – my home. Originally built as part of a European
housing exhibition, Western Harbour is now famous for being
Europe's first carbon-neutral neighbourhood. Even so, I know
I shouldn't rest on my laurels.

It's incredible how many things we can each do at home to
live more sustainably. Although a rare few sing the praises of
going completely off grid, it's not practical for the majority of
us, but you may be pleasantly surprised to hear that, as with all
things lagom, you don't need to take drastic steps – even the
smallest actions can make a big difference.

<u>Get to the source</u>

In Sweden, wind, hydro and solar power account for 52 per cent of the electricity used,[4] which places it at number one in the world for sustainable-energy use and puts it firmly on the path to becoming the first fossil-fuel-free nation. The Swedes have challenged all other countries to join the race.

These days, we're in the fortunate position of being able to choose between different energy providers. You can help your country join the movement by checking where your electricity comes from and, if necessary, switching to a company that uses more renewable sources.

KEEP YOUR HOUSE WARM
(AND COOL), SWEDISH STYLE

'When the sea is calm, every ship has a good captain.'
Swedish proverb

~~~~~

When my mother comes to visit in the winter, she always brings her thermal pyjamas – only to complain in the morning about being too hot! Swedes go to great lengths to ensure the indoor temperature is 'just right', no matter what's happening outside. Skipping about the house without a Fair Isle jumper wouldn't be possible without their practical approach to insulation. In a climate where (in the north) temperatures can plummet to -30°C (-22°F), preventing heat from escaping your home is essential. A well-insulated home has a big impact on the amount of energy we consume – not to mention keeping you toasty when the snow falls outside.

Your home-energy use

Heating accounts for 42 per cent of energy use in the average UK home. The escalating cost and environmental impact of this means that it makes sense to follow the Swedish example of checking that we're retaining heat (and, in warmer climes, keeping our homes cool) in the most efficient way. Sometimes investments are required, but they pay off in the long run.

Even small steps can help turn your home into an energy-efficient household, and it will save you pennies, too.

Layer it up

If you're not ready to make a larger insulation investment just yet, or you're lucky enough to live in a climate where extreme measures aren't necessary, adding curtains, blinds, carpets and rugs help keep the cold at bay and your home draught-free. They amp up the cosy factor, too. After all, the philosophy of lagom isn't about making things perfect, it's about putting in just the right amount of effort to ensure you're comfortable!

Wrap up

According to a report for the UK government's Department of Energy and Climate Change, dialling down the thermostat by just two degrees (from 20°C/68°F to 18°C/64°F)[5] is the number-one thing you can do to save energy at home. The report also recommended that you delay turning on your heating by one month (from October to November) and turn off radiators in unused rooms. Woolly jumpers at the ready!

Three ways to keep the heat indoors

+ Ensure your loft, walls, ceilings and floors are well insulated.
+ Eliminate draughts from windows and doors.
+ If you have a fireplace, ensure the damper is working correctly.

Shutting the door on goodbyes

Whenever guests leave our house in winter, my husband shuts the door the moment their heel passes the threshold. I'm not kidding. As a Brit used to long goodbyes, I find this excruciatingly embarrassing, but for my husband it's a force of habit. He explains that having worked tirelessly to establish an ideal temperature indoors, he's not going to let all the well-earned heat escape during a lengthy farewell! I have, of course, kept my tradition of long goodbyes, but I do it inside instead. Something to think about?

ADOPT NEW ENERGY-SAVING HABITS

It's easy to forget when we're going about our daily lives that much of what we do uses energy. These actions play a small part (but a part all the same) in using up the world's finite resources. I've spoken to many Swedes about their engagement in saving energy at home and more often than not it's a learnt behaviour from their parents and grandparents, driven by economic reasons. Now, I'm not saying you should start feeling your way around in the dark (although, of course, a Swede will tell you a few candles would be nice ...), but there are simple energy-saving habits we can all develop that will not only lead to a healthier planet but also help save money for a rainy day (or that next adventure).

Make the change

Lighting is something of a necessity – it helps us see what we're doing and (if you take the advice on pages 36–41) can create a wonderful atmosphere at home. It's little wonder that the average home now has 42 lights. But traditional light bulbs come at a cost. According to a report by Swedish Energimyndigheten (the Swedish Energy Agency),[6] they represent one-fifth of global electricity use, most of which comes from unrenewable resources. Experts advise that by changing from a traditional incandescent light bulb to an efficient LED, CFL or halogen incandescent, you'll use 25 to 80 per cent less energy, and the bulb will last up to 25 times longer.

Go natural

To reduce the amount of electricity you use, shine a light on the Swedish way of doing things – and make maximum use of natural light. Arrange furniture used for tasks requiring plenty of light nearer the window and keep the glass as unobscured as possible. Not only will your efforts be gentler on your wallet but they'll reduce your impact on the planet, too.

Did you know?

If all North American households changed from traditional incandescent light bulbs to LED, CFL or halogen incandescents, the decrease in pollution would be the same as removing a whopping 1.3 million cars from the road.

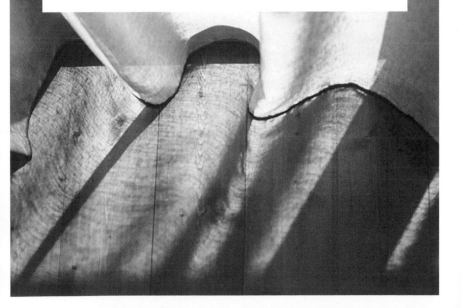

Five small energy-saving habits to adopt today

Flip the switch In our rush to get out of the house in the morning, it's easy to leave the lights on. And, really, what difference do a few light bulbs make, right? Wrong! A whopping 90 per cent of the energy used by traditional incandescent light bulbs is released through heat, and the higher the wattage, the more energy (and money) you'll save by switching off.

Unplug at the source According to the US Department of Energy, 75 per cent of our electrical output from household appliances is consumed when they are not in use. To put this in perspective, if every UK home switched off its set-top box at the source each night, the energy saved would be equivalent to the annual output of a power station. That's the equivalent of making 80 billion cups of tea.[7] *Yikes!*

Boil what you need The UK Tea and Infusions Association calculates that Brits gulp down 165 million cups of tea per day. With three out of four people admitting to overfilling the kettle each time, it's estimated that only boiling what we need could save British households 68 million pounds on energy bills a year.[8]

Stain-spot clothes In 'the good old days' when clothes were hand-washed, people would get more wear out of them. Why not remove spots with a wet cloth and air your clothes to limit the number of washes? You could even give them a good steam by hanging them beside your shower.

Skip the dryer Save energy by drying your clothes on a clothesline in the garden or on a drying rack rather than using a tumble dryer – it helps your clothes last longer, too.

SAVE WATER

Whenever I wash up or brush my teeth, my Swedish husband is there reaching to stem the flow of a running tap (yes, it's very annoying!). I've also noticed that showers are much more popular than baths in Sweden. Whether they're conscious or subconscious, these water-saving habits support the Swedish government's view that protecting water is a serious business.

Stockholm, for example, is responsible for hosting the annual World Water Week. Given that the country has almost 100,000 lakes and 11,500km (over 7,000 miles) of coastline (not including the islands), Sweden is hardly short of water. So why do Swedes go to such great lengths to preserve it? The reality is that even though 70 per cent of the Earth's surface is water, only 1 per cent of it is fit for human consumption. Alarmingly, UN statistics predict that, by 2025, two-thirds of the world's population (1.8 billion people) will live in areas with water scarcity.

Many of us aren't aware of just how much water we use every time we flush the loo, water the plants, wash the dishes or take a shower. By thinking consciously about reducing our water consumption, we can reduce the amount of energy required to process and distribute water, in turn decreasing pollution and helping to preserve this resource. In other words, it makes environmental sense for us all to step up our game and consider our water footprint.

'When the well is dry, we know the worth of water.'

Benjamin Franklin

Eight simple ways to reduce your water footprint

Turn off the tap By stemming the flow while you brush your teeth or shave, you can save up to 6 litres of water per minute (www.waterwise.org.uk).

Take five-minute showers The average bath uses 70 gallons of water compared to 10 25 gallons for a five-minute shower. By installing a reduced-flow shower head and showering for a maximum of five minutes, you'll reduce the amount of water you use by up to 80 per cent.

Fill up the machine Maximize each washing machine or dishwasher cycle by ensuring it's full before pressing the start button, and opt for the eco-cycle where possible.

Reduce the flush Toilets make up a third of household water consumption,9 making them the biggest consumer in the home. By installing a cistern displacement device, you'll reduce the amount of water per flush and still (ahem) flush away everything that needs to go.

Fix a leak A leaking tap can waste up to 26 litres of water per day, and a running toilet can consume a whopping 200 gallons per day. Time to call the plumber!

Reuse water Can't resist a soak in the bathtub? Think about collecting waste water from baths and showers to water your plants.

Keep it clean Avoid flushing chemical waste and toxins down the loo or sink. Think about exchanging your usual toiletries and cleaning products for greener versions.

Educate others Spread the word and tell family and friends. Help your children understand how important water is and how the water they use each day relates to oceans, lakes, rivers and streams.

The solar-powered outdoor shower

I've visited quite a few Swedish summer cottages with an outdoor shower. Slightly sceptical at first (I'm not a huge fan of spiders), I've grown to love them over time. Not only are they ideal for washing sandy feet after the beach but there's also something exhilarating about showering under the open sky (for a maximum of five minutes, of course). These days, solar-powered showers are creeping into the mix and are said to be one of the most eco-friendly forms of bathing. A word of warning, though – you might want to add a screen so you can truly relax!

The lagom guide to reducing our foodprint

'Food, glorious food!' Not only does it ensure
our survival but when prepared well and
enjoyed in company it also feeds the soul.
As with all consumption, it's important to limit
the effects our eating habits have on the planet.
Why not follow the Swedish example by enjoying
the odd vegetarian meal, such as *raggmunk* (potato
pancakes), de-cluttering our kitchens, taking the
odd leftover to work and composting our food
waste? In this way, we can all reduce our foodprint
and still enjoy a *härlig måltid* (tasty meal)!

PREPARING AND COOKING FOOD THE ENERGY-EFFICIENT WAY

The kitchen is known as the heart of the home for good reason – it's where we prepare food, eat and socialize. But did you know that it's also an area of the home where we waste a huge amount of energy? By making a few small changes in the way you prepare and cook food, you can save energy and time – and you'll be relishing every morsel of that homemade *äpplepaj* (apple pie) in no time.

'To eat is a necessity, but to eat intelligently is an art.'

François de La Rochefoucauld

Five ways to be energy-efficient in the kitchen

Use the right pots and pans Invest in quality cookware for improved conduction. Select the right size pan for the quantity of food you're preparing, and don't forget to keep a lid on to retain heat. You might even consider a pressure cooker, which is said to speed up cooking time by up to 70 per cent.

Keep it simple Look for recipes that require only one pot. If you're cooking pasta, think about using a metal colander on top to steam your vegetables.

Select the correct appliance Opt for smaller appliances to reduce the amount of energy required for the quantity you're preparing. When buying a new appliance, look out for energy-efficiency labels. A recent study showed that induction hobs are 32 per cent faster and use 57 per cent less energy than a gas range.[10]

Keep the oven closed It's tempting to open the oven to check on the Sunday roast – but did you know that every time you open the door, 25 per cent of the heat escapes? Try peeping through the glass instead, and use an external thermometer. You'll be tucking into lunch sooner than you think.

Use a dishwasher If you fill a modern dishwasher, it's more energy and water efficient than traditional washing up (as if you needed an excuse not to do the dishes by hand!).

Raggmunk and lingonberries, anyone?

I confess: one of my favourite meals is a nice, juicy entrecôte steak washed down with a full-bodied glass of red [*mouth waters*]. I'm not alone. It's estimated that around 2 billion people worldwide live primarily on a meat-based diet. But did you know that eating a meat-based diet consumes way more energy, water and land than a plant-based one?[11] In fact, some experts suggest that eating beef has a greater impact on our carbon footprint than driving a car! Why not exercise the philosophy of lagom and reduce your meat intake to once a week? By adding ingredients such as lingonberries (a Swedish favourite) and those needed for vegetarian dishes such as *raggmunk* (potato pancakes – see page 248) to your shopping list, we can cut our carbon footprint and still enjoy that juicy, medium-rare steak on occasion. Food for thought.

How much energy does your diet consume?

tCO2e/ person

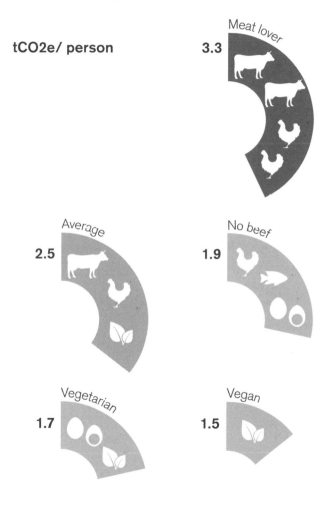

Meat lover **3.3**

Average **2.5**

No beef **1.9**

Vegetarian **1.7**

Vegan **1.5**

SWEDISH *RAGGMUNK* —
POTATO PANCAKES WITH LINGONBERRY JAM

Swedish classic *raggmunk* (potato pancakes) is quick and easy to cook and makes a perfect vegetarian meal (though it can also be served with bacon).

Serves four

+ 200g (⅔ cup) plain flour
+ 400ml (1⅓ cups) whole milk
+ 2 eggs
+ 1 tsp salt
+ black pepper (to taste)
+ 600g (1lb 3oz) potatoes (peeled)
+ 2 carrots (peeled)
+ 30g (2 tbsp) butter
+ a jar of lingonberry jam

1. Preheat the oven to 150°C/300°F/gas mark 2.

2. Combine the flour and 200ml of the milk in a bowl and whisk until the texture is smooth.

3. Pour in the rest of the milk, then add the eggs, salt and pepper, and whisk into a smooth batter.

4. Roughly grate the potatoes and carrots, and stir into the batter.

5. Melt the butter in a frying pan.

6. Keeping the pan on a high heat, add a large dollop of the batter to the frying pan (the amount you add depends on how large you would like your pancake – we tend to add 2 tablespoons of batter per pancake).

7. Fry the pancake for approximately 1 minute on each side or until golden.

8. Keep the pancake warm on a baking tray in the oven and repeat the process until all the batter has been used up (you can fry more than one at a time depending on the size of your pan).

9. Once all the pancakes are done, serve with a dollop of lingonberry jam. If you are unable to find lingonberry jam, they also taste great with soured cream and snipped chives.

HOW TO REDUCE FOOD WASTE

Ever come across a putrid cucumber lurking at the back of the fridge? Or an outdated tin of tomato soup in the cupboard? Have you ever scraped leftovers into the bin? You're not alone. According to the 2012 report 'Food waste volumes in Sweden', households generated the largest amount of food waste (even surpassing supermarkets and restaurants). According to the US Environmental Protection Agency, Americans tossed away 38 million tonnes of food in 2014. Alarmingly, 95 per cent of this food waste ends up in landfill or a combustion facility, contributing to increased methane emissions.[12] Eeeek!

With 35 per cent of this wastage unnecessary, *matavfall* (food waste) is something the Swedes take very seriously indeed. In many parts of the country, the local authorities supply eco-friendly paper bags for it, which they then collect and convert into biogas to run city buses. Today, Sweden is the global leader in food-waste reduction.

We all inevitably end up with scraps after a meal or spoiled food in the fridge, but this doesn't mean it needs to go to waste. If we all adopt new strategies in the way we shop, store food and handle leftovers, we, too, can help conserve energy and save money. There are plenty of ways to ensure that even the limpest carrots and weeks-old potatoes don't end up in landfills, starting with your weekly shop!

'Love and food are meant for sharing, not wasting.'

Anonymous

Plan your grocery shopping

Eat what you have in your fridge before buying more.

Each time you shop, make a note of how many meals you will need to buy.

Plan and jot down the ingredients for each meal.

Plan to eat a meal made up of leftovers at least once or twice a week.

Make a list of the type and quantity of food you need to buy, as well as which meals they'll cover (if more than one). Check that you don't already have these items in stock.

Once at the supermarket, stick to the list and don't be sidetracked by promotions and offers.

Keep food in sight

If your cupboards and refrigerator are packed with produce, it's hard to see what you have, which means you're more likely to forget what you have and waste food. Channel the Swedes' minimalist, clutter-free approach by keeping stocks to a manageable amount and ensuring everything is well organized and in view. Using see-through, airtight containers like Mason jars and eco-friendly boxes helps to keep food fresh and clearly visible.

Store in the right way

It's easy to chuck items in the fridge, thinking they'll stay fresher for longer, but this isn't always the case. Bananas, for example, fare better out on the counter (the fridge slows the ripening process and can lead to rotting). Lagom is about taking time to do things in the right way, so take a moment to read up on the correct way to store each item you buy. Not only will they last longer but they'll taste just right, too!

Yesterday's leftovers – today's *pyttipanna*

Despite our best efforts, leftovers can be unavoidable. But what to do with them? After all, cold pork chops and limp potatoes don't look nearly as enticing as they did with that glass of red the night before …

Due to their limited means, our ancestors were masters at food preservation and waste reduction. In Sweden, the popular dish *pyttipanna,* or 'small pieces in a pan', was traditionally devised from a hodgepodge of leftovers. Today the dish is made from diced potatoes, scraps of meat, onions and leftover vegetables, tossed together in a pan and then fried. Why not give it a go with the contents of your fridge? For a truly Swedish touch, serve with fried egg and pickled beetroot, then garnish with snipped chives to turn yesterday's leftovers into today's gourmet meal.

Smaklig måltid ('Bon appétit')!

Start a compost heap

No matter how resourceful you are, there will always be a few scraps left over. My Swedish father-in-law will tell you that if you have a garden, composting is an incredible way to turn vegetable peel, coffee grounds and eggshells from landfill fodder into soil packed with nutrients.

COMPOST HEAP 101

▽

Starting a compost heap can be as simple as tossing potato peel, eggshells, grass clippings and dead leaves into a pile at the back of your garden. Or you can go the more professional route and invest in a state-of-the-art compost bin. Either way, the process is pretty much the same.

+ Stick to items that are 100 per cent natural or have 'lived'.

+ Try to ensure that your compost is made up of elements that are moist and dry, green and brown.

+ Cut or shred scraps into small pieces and keep the heap moist.

+ Air your compost once a week with a pitchfork or other means.

+ Once decomposed, the soil is good to go – and your garden will be positively blooming in no time!

TAP INTO YOUR INNER FARMER

As a child, I spent a lot of weekends at my parents' allotment, and I can't say my sisters and I were filled with joy at the idea. But three things remain with me to this day: seeing the rows of sweet peas, marrows and runner beans; the delicious gooseberry fool my mother made from the produce in summertime, and the day I trod barefoot on a slug. Swedes are very fond of their *kolonilott* (allotments), which also sometimes come with a dwelling akin to a small summer cottage; which people enjoy from early spring to late autumn (depending on when the water supply is cut off to prevent the pipes from freezing). Not everyone has the time (or money) for an extra plot of land, but there's an exciting movement under way.

Growing your own herbs, flowers and vegetables is gaining in popularity in Swedish cities. City dwellers are using the space they have (small backyards, balconies, vertical gardens) and making use of the urban-farm initiative – in which local authorities offer planter boxes – in parks and even in converted garages.

If you have a large garden, you're in luck. But for those of you with smaller outdoor spaces, it's incredible what you can cultivate on your balcony or even through cracks in the pavement. Why not join the movement and create your own edible landscape? Not only will you benefit from locally produced, eco-friendly fruit and veg (if cultivated in the right way) but you'll also avoid chemicals and reduce your carbon footprint.

257 — Lagom in the wider world

Five ways to farm in a small space

Vertical garden When space is tight, the only way is up! All you need is a fence or blank wall, and you're already on your way to a vertical, edible garden.

Espaliered fruit tree Who says you can't have an orchard in a 4-metre (13-foot) -square backyard? Specially grafted fruit trees are designed to take up a small horizontal space – and they will bear as much fruit as you can eat by autumn.

Windowsill box Why not fit windowsill boxes and tend to your salad leaves and herbs through your open window? (No wellies necessary!)

Windowsill Make the most of a sunny spot by the window to grow herbs, tomatoes and other summer-salad essentials.

Indoor grow lights If your home is relatively dark and without outdoor space, there's still a grow-your-own option. Source seeds and plants that thrive under a grow light and do a little gardening from the comfort of your sitting room.

'To forget how to dig the earth and tend the soil is to forget ourselves.'

Mahatma Gandhi

VERTICAL GARDEN HACK

▽

A vertical garden doesn't have to be any more complicated than hanging a cotton shoe rack on a blank wall and planting a selection of your favourite herbs in the pockets.

The shared herb garden/vegetable patch

The majority of Swedish apartment blocks have access to a garden for entertaining, bicycle storage and general enjoyment of outdoor life. When visiting friends, I've often also clocked small vegetable patches, featuring rows of herbs such as rosemary, thyme and mint, which residents are invited to pick for their own use.

If you have access to a shared outdoor space, why not start a community garden? It won't require much work if the maintenance is shared, and it's amazing how quickly herbs replenish – so there's always enough to go around.

From kitchen scraps to urban jungle

If potato-peel pie or banana-skin smoothies aren't quite your thing (yet!), and you don't have room for a compost heap, you could consider turning everyday scraps into an urban oasis. You can find all kinds of YouTube clips on how to nurture plants from scraps (and a few starter suggestions on pages 262–263). In our house, my kids and I find it incredibly inspiring to watch an old lettuce leaf or garlic clove transform into a lush new plant. Plus, it won't cost you a penny!

Three plants you can grow from kitchen scraps

+ Spring onion Use leftover white roots and place standing up in a container with a little water in the bottom, so only the roots are wet. A new shoot should start to appear within three to five days. Simply cut as needed and refresh the water once a week to keep your plant healthy.

For outdoor gardening, make sure you observe the correct season for planting and harvesting.

+ Garlic clove Pull off a clove from the bulb, then plant it in a large pot with the papery wrapper still on and the pointed end facing upwards (it should be at least 5cm from the rim and 2.5cm deep in the soil). Place it in direct sunlight and keep moist. When small shoots start to appear cut them down to the base. Eight to ten months later the shoots will start to turn brown and you'll know it's time to harvest your garlic bulb. Hang the bulb to dry for one week in a cool place before consuming.

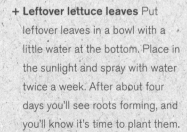

+ Leftover lettuce leaves Put leftover leaves in a bowl with a little water at the bottom. Place in the sunlight and spray with water twice a week. After about four days you'll see roots forming, and you'll know it's time to plant them.

THE BRANTMARK FAMILY
ELDERFLOWER CORDIAL

▽

Every June in Sweden, wild elderflower bushes burst into life with delicate white blossoms. I'm particularly fond of my brother-in-law Johan and his wife Monica's homemade elderflower cordial, which they serve at midsummer.

Makes approx. 2.5 litres (5 pints)

+ 35–40 freshly picked European elderflowers (*Sambucus nigra*), stems removed ★
+ 3–4 lemons (preferably organic)

+ 1.5 litres (6 cups) water
+ 1.5kg (6 cups) caster sugar
+ 50g (¼ cup) citric acid

1. Some recipes tell you to rinse the flowers, but Johan and Monica think it diminishes the flavour. Instead, shake the flowers to remove insects.

2. Place the flowers in a large bowl (capacity 4 litres/8½ pints).

3. Rinse the lemons, slice thinly (leaving the rind on) and add to the bowl.

4. Pour the water into a saucepan and bring to the boil.

5. Add the sugar to the saucepan and stir with a wooden spoon until the sugar has dissolved.

6. Remove the pan from the heat and stir in the citric acid.

7. Pour the hot syrup over the flowers and lemons in the bowl and stir if needed.

8. Cover the bowl with a lid or cling film and leave in the fridge or similar cool place for three to four days.

9. Strain the liquid through a colander or a thin tea towel, depending on how clear you would like your cordial to be (the texture will make no difference to the taste).

To serve
Blend the cordial with up to five parts water (depending on your taste) and add ice for a truly refreshing drink. You can also use the cordial in fruit-salad dressing, cake flavouring, ice pops and even your favourite tipple for a true taste of summer.

To store
The best way to make it last all summer is to place it in the freezer. It will remain relatively soft, so it will be easy to scoop out when required and it thaws quickly in water.

* There are many different varieties of elderflower, some not fit for human consumption. Always use the European elderflower (*Sambucus nigra*) variety for elderflower cordial, characterized by flat clusters of yellowish-white flowers with a white inner.

Always consult an expert before consuming hand-picked produce.

Home-flavoured schnapps and brews

No celebration at my father-in-law's house would be complete without home-flavoured schnapps. There's something extra-special about the infusion of wormwood, dill, bog myrtle or St John's wort in aquavit that makes the nectar taste especially good. The clear recycled bottles and charming homemade labels (often featuring a sketch of the herb in question) add to the occasion, too.

If you fancy channelling your inner biologist but are not so keen on the strong stuff, why not try brewing your own beer? Microbreweries have been popping up in Sweden faster than you can say '*Öl, tack,*' ('Beer, please') and this is also catching on in the Swedish home. The beauty of home-brews is that they're sustainably produced, organic – and you can't get more 'local'! In our time-poor world, they don't take a lot of effort to produce, plus, I'm told the creative process is truly rewarding.

If you'd like to give it a go, there are plenty of online tutorials offering know-how into making both home-flavoured schnapps and homemade beer. You'll be enjoying a shot or a swift one fresh from the keg in no time!

The lagom guide
to eco daily life

It's not just personal transport that contributes
to greenhouse-gas emissions. When we buy
something new, it often travels thousands of miles
to reach our home. Plus, there's the energy (and
waste) involved in creating the item in the first
place. Over the past decade, I've noticed a growing
trend in Sweden: more economically savvy Swedes
are buying secondhand, participating in lending
schemes and repairing what's already out there.
I promise that once you get into it, you'll also
wonder why you bought so much new!

ECO-FRIENDLY TRANSPORT

In Sweden, running errands on a bicycle is second nature. It's simply a more practical way to travel. Sometimes, though, an ordinary bike isn't up to the task – the distance is too far, you have too much to carry or the weather gods are really not on your side (no matter how 'weather appropriately' you dress).

On those days, it's tempting to hop into the comfort of your car, whack up the heating and sing along to the radio. After all, the car is waiting outside your door, and you don't have to study a timetable or wait at a windy bus stop. But if we consider the carbon emissions, there are many more environmentally friendly ways to get about.

The freight bike

Also known as a cargo or box bike, a freight bike is a specially adapted bicycle with a front carrier designed to help you transport bigger loads without a car. From children and groceries to work supplies and Christmas trees – this nifty bicycle is a super-efficient way to get your load across town without adding to your carbon footprint. Plus, it gives your quads a great workout. Who needs a gym anyway?

The electric bicycle

The other day, I was racing along a bicycle path in Malmö (late, as usual) when an elderly gentleman casually pedalled past me without so much as breaking into a sweat. I was taken aback and, being rather competitive, pedalled harder in an effort to regain my position. But the guy steadily broke away from me and pedalled off into the sunset. It was only later that I realized he'd been on an electric bicycle, or e-bike.

So what exactly is an e-bike? It's a modified or custom-built bicycle complete with pedals, but it runs on an electric motor. Riders can choose how much effort they'd like to exert, from propelling themselves like on a normal pushbike to using the full motor drive so they don't need to work at all, which is ideal for longer distances.

Given that it runs off a battery, does it just get you across town more quickly or does it actually reduce your carbon footprint? While it's emission-free to ride an e-bike, there is the energy used to build it and keep it charged. Plus there's the battery changing and disposal to consider. But if the distances you cover day to day are simply not possible on a traditional bike, an e-bike is significantly more environmentally friendly than a car or motorcycle. Plus, it's way cheaper to run and, given the traffic, you'll likely arrive sooner, too.

Use cars more efficiently

Even for the bike-mad Swede, sometimes there's just no getting around the fact that we need to use a car – whether it's due to distance, time or logistics. Even so, there are ways to reduce the impact. Commuters, for example, can save money and help to cut carbon emissions by sharing the journey with colleagues. If no one else travels the same route as you or you're going on a one-off trip, register your name on a rideshare website to find like-minded people heading in the same direction. Not only can you save a fortune on travel but you might also turn a tedious solo journey into an all-singing, all-dancing road trip (or simply enjoy a little company along the way).

Many of my Swedish friends have also opted to use official carpool schemes rather than invest in their own car. Carpools are similar to renting a car, the difference being that they're designed to make it easy to pick up a car for a few hours and pay for one-off use (including mileage and time), and they're steadily popping up all over urban areas. A carpool is likely to be convenient for you if you live in a city – you'll enjoy an immaculate vehicle (unlike ours, which has cornflakes on the backseat) and cut your carbon footprint. And if you don't need regular access, you'll save cash, too.

Electric cars

Electric cars and hybrids are a hot topic in the automotive industry. At the Swedbank Nordic Energy Summit in Oslo in 2016, author and entrepreneur Tony Seba predicted that all new road vehicles will be running entirely on electricity by 2030. How much more environmentally friendly this will be compared to using classic diesel or petrol-run cars depends on how green the electricity source is. However, once on the road, even a hybrid will spew out less carbon dioxide and nitrogen oxide than these traditional options, making it a greener choice overall. By investing in a form of electric car, you'll also be supporting the industries working towards a more eco-friendly world. And as renewable energies continue to progress, there's hope that the cars will come on leaps and bounds.

Public transport

The ultimate 'lift share' is usually waiting just at the end of our road: public transport. The thought of a bus might immediately conjure up black fumes spluttering from an exhaust, but these days they're starting to clean up their act. Governments around the world are working hard to make buses, trains and trams greener and more accessible in a bid to reduce the number of gas-guzzling vehicles on the road. In Sweden, renewable fuels make up 67 per cent of buses' consumption,[13] and with a government target to ensure all buses run on renewable, environmentally friendly fuel by 2025, it's certainly a more eco-friendly way to get about than driving. The key to optimizing transport systems, though, is to ensure that they aren't running around empty. In other words, to make an impact, we all need to use buses and trains more often.

Enjoy a moment's silence!

In many Swedish cities it's illegal to sit in a stationary car with your engine running for more than a minute or two. Many modern cars have stop/start technology, but if yours doesn't and you're waiting for a friend or sitting in a traffic jam, why not kill your engine for a few minutes? You'll lower your carbon emissions and enjoy a little silence.

ECO-FRIENDLY SHOPPING

According to the IVL Swedish Environmental Research Institute, every mobile phone produces a whopping 86kg (190lb) of waste during manufacture. And that's before the waste that is incurred after it breaks or we upgrade to a new model. Eeeek! 'We can all do more to stop and think before we buy something new,' advises Swedish environmental educator Ann Nerlund. 'It's hard to resist trends, advertising and everyday temptations – but once you start to think more consciously about the impact of each new item you buy, it becomes an easier decision.'

Buying less doesn't mean we need to go without, though. There are plenty of ways to acquire what you need without doing unnecessary harm to the planet.

Buy greener

A study by the European Commission found that 40 per cent of Swedes buy an item with an eco-label each month, placing them at the top of the European ranking for eco-label purchasing. Eco-labels, or green stickers, are designed to make it easier for shoppers to consider the environment when making a buying decision. By seeking out eco-labelled items, you're making a conscious decision to reduce your effect on the planet. And since they're free of chemicals, it'll benefit your health (and the health of the people that make the product, too).

Buy secondhand

The Swedish vintage-clothing market has grown dramatically over the past few years, with many people opting for secondhand over new.

By giving a garment a new lease of life, you're saving on the energy it takes to produce and ship an item, not to mention the fact that you will be sporting an item that no one else has.

There's no need to stop at your threads, though. Swedes love a bargain from a *loppis* (flea market) and happily scour local online sites, markets, secondhand stores and swap shops to find whatever it is they're looking for. They also get their children involved, helping them sell their own toys and clothes, and buying from stalls at *barnloppis* (children's flea markets). If you haven't already discovered the satisfaction of it, why not give it a go? You can find pretty much anything you need if you look hard enough.

Four items that are best to buy used

Bicycles New rides can be pricey, so pick one up secondhand. With a little elbow grease, you'll be cycling to work and saving money in no time.

Children's clothes and toys Our little munchkins get taller and cuter by the day, but this also means they grow out of many items before they're worn out (or sometimes even used at all). This means there are stacks of bargains to be found secondhand, and many of them look as good as new.

Jewellery Not many people are aware that jewellery has a fairly low secondhand value. This means you can often buy the most beautiful pieces for less than you'd find in a store. It also means the piece has a history, which makes it unique.

Sports equipment and musical instruments Let's face it: when we (or our children) try a new sport, we hardly need shiny new equipment fit for a pro. Why not buy what you need used? Skis, tennis rackets, violins and more can all be picked up for a song and easily given a new lease of life with a little TLC. And if that doesn't work, we can always blame 'faulty equipment' when we don't perform as well as we should!

Share and share alike

My family and I are lucky enough to have the most amazing neighbours. I can't tell you how many times we knock on their door to borrow something. They're always eager to help, and I'm relieved when they come round for the same reason.

This type of 'borrowing' has been enjoyed since mankind began. It's only now that it's being seen with fresh eyes, with more sophisticated reuse schemes being put in place. In my adopted hometown of Malmö, for example, there are many sharing schemes. Members of the public can hire tools from the library and sports equipment from Fritidsbanken (The Leisure Bank) for free. It's well worth looking out for sharing schemes in your community. Not only will they save you money but they'll also help reduce your carbon footprint.

Darn those socks!

Darning socks has long been a thing of the past. These days a sock with a hole in is immediately confined to the waste-paper basket (especially in Sweden, where the chances of someone seeing your toe poking out is relatively high – see pages 42–43). In fact, we're guilty of chucking out just about anything that's broken: appliances, toys, household items – all of which will likely end up as landfill.

But, in Sweden, this is starting to change. The government is planning a series of tax breaks and VAT cuts designed to make it cheaper for people to repair items such as washing machines, bikes and clothes. And Swedish brands such as Nudie Jeans are offering customers an onsite repair service. 'We don't believe "throwaway" and "jeans" are words that belong together,' says Eliina Brinkberg, environmental manager at Nudie Jeans. 'We believe in a slower consumption, of using clothes for a long time, and we want to give our customers the possibility of consuming in a far more sustainable way.'

So, next time you're about to chuck something in the bin, stop and think, Can this be repaired? Who knows? You might find yourself darning socks before you know it.

Conclusion

'The right amount is best.'
Swedish proverb

~~~~~~~

Writing this book has been quite a journey. I've lived in
Sweden with my Swedish husband for 13 years, and my
children attend Swedish schools, so I thought I knew
everything there was to know about Swedes and the lagom
lifestyle they lead. In fact, I believed that my fast-paced
'London girl' persona had quietly taken a back seat, and
that there was a calmer version of me in her place. After all,
I take time to *umgås* (hang out) and *fika* (take coffee breaks).
I try not to work on holiday, and my husband and I share
parenting and household chores 50:50. I even ride my bike
in the snow. That's pretty Swedish behaviour, right?

Over the past six months, I've had the pleasure of talking
to many Swedes about topics related to lagom. This includes
family, friends, experts and even strangers in cafés (lagom turns
out to be a great ice-breaker if you ever find yourself grappling
for conversation with a quieter Swede). Lagom evokes animated
reactions, and it seems everyone has something to say about it.
What struck me most was just how automatic much of lagom is
to the Swedes. Slowing down and taking time to do things in a
fuss-free way is as instinctive to them as enjoying meatballs and
mash or buying furniture from IKEA.

But as the adage goes: 'You can take the girl out of London, but you can't take London out of the girl.' As a Brit living in Sweden, there are habits I simply can't (or would rather not) shake off. And perhaps you feel the same. But do you know what? That's totally OK, because the beauty of a lagom approach is that it's a very personal thing. It's about finding a balance that works for you. If you want that piece of cake, eat it. If you want to swing from the chandeliers, swing, by all means (although the safety-conscious Swedes might advise against it). And you don't need to punish yourself for the next month by embarking on a strict diet or abstaining from espresso martinis.

Lagom isn't about denying yourself life's pleasures; it's about enjoying everything in moderation – in a healthy, balanced way. And perhaps, like me, you'll find that experimenting with lagom and making subtle changes to your routine will not only bring a sense of equilibrium to your life; it will also bring you a greater feeling of calm and contentment.

Endnotes Part 1

1. McMains, S. & Kastner, S., 'Interactions of top-down and bottom-up mechanisms in human visual cortex', *Journal of Neuroscience*, Jan 2011, 31(2); doi:10.1523/JNEUROSCI.3766-10.2011

2. Nieuwenhuis, M., Knight, C. et al., 'The relative benefits of green versus lean office space: Three field experiments', *Journal of Applied Psychology*: Sept 2014, 20(3), pp.199–214:

3. Van den Berg M., Maas J., et al., 'Autonomic nervous system responses to viewing green and built settings' *International Journal of Environmental Research*, 2015, 12(12); doi:10.3390/ijerph121215026

4. Harb, F., Hidalgo, M.P., & Martau, B., 'Lack of exposure to natural light in the workspace is associated with physiological, sleep and depressive symptoms', *Chronobiology International*, Apr 2015, 32(3):, pp.368–75.

5. Old-generation LED light bulbs only change intensity, but new LED light bulbs change both colour temperature and intensity.

6. https://www.rugdoctor.co.uk/about-us/news/what-lies-beneath-the-dirty-truth-about-our-carpets

7. Hysing, M., Pallesen, S., et al., 'Sleep and use of electronic devices in adolescence', *BMJ*, 2015, 5(1)

8. Jansky, L. et al., 'Immune system of cold-exposed and cold-adapted humans' *European Journal of Applied Physiology*, 1996, 72(5-6) pp. 445-50

9. Shevchuk N., 'Adapted cold shower as a potential treatment for depression', *Medical Hypotheses*, 2008, 70(5), pp. 995-1001

10. Laukkanen T., Khan H., Zaccardi F. & Laukkanen J.A., 'Association between sauna bathing and fatal cardiovascular and All-cause mortality events'.*JAMA Internal Medicine*. 2015, 175(4) pp. 542-548; doi:10.1001/jamainternmed.2014.8187

11. Richardson, M., Cormack, A., et al., '30 days wild: Development and evaluation of a large-scale nature engagement campaign to improve well-being' PLOS, Feb 2016; https://doi.org/10.1371/journal.pone.0149777

12. Uusitupa M., et al, 'Effects of an isocaloric healthy Nordic diet on insulin sensitivity, lipid profile and inflammation markers in metabolic syndrome' *Journal of International Medicine,* March 2013; doi:10.1111/joim.12044

13. Heyman, L., Axling, U., Blanco, N., et al., 'Evaluation of beneficial metabolic effects of berries in high-fat fed C57BL/6J mice', *Journal of Nutrition and Metabolism*, Jan 2014; doi:10.1155/2014/403041

14. Martin, A., Goryakin, Y., & Suhrcke, M. , 'Does active commuting improve psychological wellbeing? Longitudinal evidence from eighteen waves of the British Household Panel Survey' *Preventive Medicine*, Dec 2014; https://doi.org/10.1016/j.ypmed.2014.08.023

15. Pencavel, J., 'The productivity of working hours' Stanford University, Apr 2014; http://ftp.iza.org/dp8129.pdf

16. Rosenberg, J., Maximov, I.I., Reske, M., Grinberg, F. & Shah, N.J., '"Early to bed, early to rise": Diffusion tensor imaging identifies chronotype-specificity' *NeuroImage*, Jan 2014; https://doi.org/10.1016/j.neuroimage.2013.07.086

17. Randler, C., 'Proactive people are morning people' *Journal of Applied Social Psychology,* 2009, 39(12); doi:10.1111/j.1559-1816.2009.00549.x

18. Elias, C., 'Morning people happier and healthier than night owls', University of Toronto Faculty of Arts & Science, June 2012; http://www.artsci.utoronto.ca/main/newsitems/morning-people-happier

19. Hunter, E. M. & Wu, C., 'Give me a *better* break: Choosing workday break activities to maximize resource recovery' *Journal of Applied Psychology*, 101(2), Feb 2016; doi: 10.1037/apl0000045

20. Data analysed from app DESKTIME

21. *Cornell Chronicle*, Sept 1999; http://www.news.cornell.edu/stories/1999/09/onscreen-break-reminder-boosts-productivity

22. Suomen Akatemia (Academy of Finland), 'Listening to music lights up the whole brain' *ScienceDaily*, Dec 2011; https://www.sciencedaily.com/releases/2011/12/111205081731.htm

23. Journal of Sleep and Sleep Disorders Research, 2013, 36(1); http://www.journalsleep.org/resources/documents/2013AbstractSupplement.pdf

24. *Cornell Chronicle*, Oct 2004; http://www.news.cornell.edu/stories/2004/10/warm-offices-linked-fewer-typing-errors-higher-productivity

25. Nieuwenhuis, M., Knight, C., Postmes, T. & Haslam, S. A., 'The relative benefits of green versus lean office space: Three field experiments'. *Journal of Experimental Psychology,* Sept 2014, 20(3), doi; 10.1037/xap0000024

26. https://www.glassdoor.com/press/glassdoor-survey-reveals-average-american-employee-takes-earned-vacationpaid-time-61-report-working-vacation/

27. de Bloom, J., Geurts, S. & Kompier, M., 'Vacation (after-) effects on employee health and wellbeing, and the role of vacation activities, experiences and sleep' *Journal of Happiness Studies*, Apr 2013, 14(2); https://doi.org/10.1007/s10902-012-9345-3

Endnotes Part 2

1. Mostofsky, E., Rice, M.S., et al., 'Habitual coffee consumption and risk of heart failure: A dose-response meta-analysis' *Circulation: Heart Failure,* July 2012, 5(4), pp.401–5

2   Hedström, A.K., Mowry, E.M., et al., 'High consumption of coffee is associated with decreased multiple sclerosis risk', *Journal of Neurology Neurosurgery and Psychiatry,* March 2016; doi:10.1136/jnnp-2015-312176

3. Rosendahl, A.H., Perks, C. M., Zeng, L., et al., 'Caffeine and caffeic acid inhibit growth and modify estrogen receptor and insulin-like growth factor/Receptor levels in human breast cancer', *Clinical Cancer Research,* March 2015; doi:10.1158/1078-0432.CCR-14-1748

4. Gottman, J.M. & Levenson, R. W. , 'A two-factor model for predicting when a couple will divorce' *Family Processes Journal,* 41(1), 2002, pp. 83-96.

5. The Knot 2015 Real Weddings Survey

6. Francis, A.M. & Mialon, H.M., '"A diamond is forever" and other fairy tales: The relationship between wedding expenses and marriage duration', Sept 2014, available at SSRN; https://ssrn.com/abstract=2501480

7. Morrison, M. & Roese, N.J., 'Regrets of the typical American: Findings from a nationally representative sample', *SAGE Journal, Social Psychological and Personality Science,* 2(6), March 2011.

8. Sylva, K., Melhuish, E., Sammons, P., Siraj-Blatchford, I., & Taggart, B. 'Early childhood matters: evidence from the effective preschool and primary education project' Oxford, Routledge 2010.

9. Caldera, Y.M., O'Brian, et al., 'Children's play preferences, construction play with blocks, and visual-spatial skills: Are they related?', *International Journal of Behavioural Development,* 1999, 23(4), pp. 855–72.

10. Nolan, G., McFarland, A., Zajicek, J. & Waliczek, T., 'The effects of nutrition education and gardening on attitudes, preferences, and knowledge of Minority Second to Fifth Graders in the Rio Grande valley toward fruit and vegetables', *HortTechnology,* June 2012, 22(3), pp.299–304.

11. Sherwin, J.C., Reacher, M.H., Keogh, R.H., et al, 'The association between time spent outdoors and myopia in children and adolescents', *Ophthalmology,* Oct 2012, 119(10), pp. 2141–2151.

12. Blackwell, S., 'Impacts of long-term forest school programmes on children's resilience, confidence and wellbeing', Wordpress, June 2016

13. Suggate, S.P., Schaughency, E.A. & Reese, E., 'Children learning to read later catch up to children reading earlier', *Early Childhood Research Quarterly,* 28(1), 2013, pp.33–48.

14. Wikipedia: https://en.wikipedia.org/wiki/Hen_%28pronoun%29

Endnotes Part 3

1. Anik, L., Aknin, L. B, Norton, M. I. & Dunn, E.W., 'Feeling good about giving: The benefits (and costs) of self-interested charitable behavior', Harvard Business School, 2009

2. Wike, R., Stokes B., & Simmons K., 'Europeans fear wave of refugees will mean more terrorism, fewer jobs', *Pew Research Center,* July 2016

3. 'Reducing wasted food and packaging: A guide for food services and restaurants', United States Environmental Protection Agency, 2015

4. Eurostat, news release, Feb 2016 www.sweden.se

5. Palmer, J., Terry, N. & Pope, P., 'How much energy could be saved by making small changes to everyday household behaviours?', *Cambridge Architectural Research,* Nov 2012

6. 'Goodnight light bulb: The Swedish Energy Agency's guide to the new light', Energimyndigheten, March 2011

7. Office of Communications (Ofcom) 'The UK Communications Market Report', Aug 2008

8. C0337 Energy Saving Trust 'At Home with Water', July 2013

9. Foekema, H.; van Thiel, L., Lettinga, B. Watergebruik Thuis 2007 [in Dutch]; Vewin Vereniging van waterbedrijven in Nederland: Amsterdam, The Netherlands, 2008.

10. Paul Scheckel, *Home Energy Pros,* June 2016

11. Pimentel, D. & Pimentel, M., 'Sustainability of meat-based and plant-based diets and the environment' *The American Journal of Clinical Nutrition,* Sep 2003, 78(3), 660S-663S

12. United States Environmental Protection Agency, 2014

13. Xylia, M. and Silveira, S., 'On the road to fossil-free public transport: The case of Swedish bus fleets', *Energy Policy,* Feb 2016; https://doi.org/10.1016/j.enpol.2016.02.024

Index

Page references in *italics* indicate photographs or illustrations.

Picture credits by page number

Thank you

It's quite unbelievable how many people have contributed to this book – it's truly been a team effort! To mention them one by one would require a whole new chapter. Many have entrusted me with tips, knowledge, personal experiences, DIY ideas and recipes over the past few months; others have opened their hearts and minds to make me feel welcome in my wonderful adopted home of Sweden. Some have been there for me over a lifetime.

I have tried my best to thank everyone individually. However, I would like to emphasize just how grateful I am for the love, support and words of encouragement. It has been 'just right!'

ABOUT THE AUTHOR

Niki Brantmark is the creator of My Scandinavian Home, an interior design blog inspired by her life in Malmö, Sweden, where she lives with her husband and three children. Originally from London, Niki has an MA in psychology from the University of Edinburgh and is the author of *Modern Pastoral* and *The Scandinavian Home*.